The Isle Full of Noises:

Modern Chinese Poetry from Taiwan

Modern Asian Literature Series

The Isle Full of Noises
Modern Chinese Poetry from Taiwan

Edited and Translated by
Dominic Cheung

New York
Columbia University Press
1987

The Press gratefully acknowledges the financial assistance of the College of Letters, Arts and Sciences of the University of Southern California in the publication of this book.

Library of Congress Cataloging-in-Publication Data

The Isle full of noises.

(Modern Asian literature series)
Bibliography: p.
1. Chinese poetry—Taiwan—Translations into English.
2. English poetry—Translation from Chinese.
I. Cheung, Dominic. II. Series.
PL2658.E3I85 1987   895.1'15'080951249   86-13614
ISBN 0-231-06402-0

Columbia University Press
New York   Guildford, Surrey
Copyright © 1987 Columbia University Press

Printed in the United States of America

For my mother and
elegance promised

Modern Asian Literature Series

Contents

Introduction

Modern Chinese poetry from Taiwan no more represents a continuation of the mainland's new poetics than it does a break from its own painful, local tradition. Taiwan has its own poetry, with its own Chinese identity. From the 1894 defeat of the Manchurian empire until after 1945, during which time its poets wrote in both the Chinese and Japanese languages, the Japanese undoubtedly favored Taiwanese poetry written in Japanese. Even if written in Chinese, poems written in the old *wen-yen* (classical) language were favored above those written in the *pai-hua* (vernacular). Those engaged in new poetry are regarded by the Japanese as more liberal in thought and rebellious in action.

However, concerning the poets writing in classical Chinese, it cannot be concluded that they yielded to the Japanese oppressors. For example, the literary arguments between Chang Wo-chun,[1] a modern, and Lien Ya-t'ang,[2] a classicist, were polemics waged between two patriots. Chang Wo-chun, a then new poet who had received his college education in Peking, had returned to live in Taiwan upon its liberation from the Japanese. Before leaving the mainland, he had vigorously criticized the callousness and sterility found in the classical writers' works, writing such articles as "How Horrendous is Taiwanese Literature," "Farewell to Dr. Ku," and "Let Us Take Down this Dilapidated Temple in Withered Weeds." Not only do these articles attack the practices of classical writers, they reveal in Chang a strong craving for a Chinese identity, and thus distinguish him as a warrior of resistance.

When Dr. Sun Yat-sen, founder of the Chinese Republic, died in 1925, the news of his death so saddened and shocked local Taiwanese that they started to organize a meeting in memory of their national father. The Japanese reluctantly permitted the assembly, however allowed no obituaries or elegies. In fact, the only elegy planned to be read was Chang Wo-chun's, in which he says,

> Oh! Once the great star has fallen,
> The East Asian universe suddenly darkens;
> Our most respected great man,
> Did you forever leave us on March 12, at 9:30 in the morning?
> Forty million citizens are wearing sad faces because of your death;
> When the news came to this island,
> Everyone was desperate and full of sorrow, as if each had lost his own soul;
> Looking west, to the mainland,
> They shed tears.[3]

Taiwanese identification with the people of the mainland is obvious in this poem. "When they look west," their tears fall not only for Sun Yat-sen's death but also from the hope and despair they've endured while waiting for Sun to liberate them from Japanese rule.

Early precursors of the new Taiwanese poetry, published from 1923 to 1937 in *The Taiwan People's News,* include Shih Wen-ch'i, Yang Yung-p'ing, Chang Wo-chung, Yang Hau, and Lai Ho. The problem with their poetry has not so much to do with their lack of national sentiments or emotions, as with their inability to find an appropriate poetic language or voice. Their dilemma, however, is understandable: most of them had just released themselves from the classical language; worse still, they were subject to the Japanese publishers' whims spoken of earlier, whereby Japanese was considered a more important language. Chang Wo-chung's critical essays, for example, reveal a much stronger voice than his poems, which some regard as no more than separated lines of prose.[4] However, we must bear in mind that many of these poets wrote in Chinese as their second or third language, depending upon Taiwanese as their native or Japanese as their first language.

Toward the end of World War II the situation changed, so that more poets and writers began to write in Japanese. In fact, even with the outbreak of the Pacific war in 1937, the Japanese forbade the use of Chinese. During a temporary silence of Chinese writers, many left for the mainland; many others simply stopped writing. Meanwhile there emerged a new generation of poets, with a sharp political consciousness and keen poetical sensibilities. Though they wrote in Japanese, their poems are nonetheless "Chinese." Consider, for example, Wu Yung-fu's "Mother Country," part of which is quoted here:

> The mother country which I have never seen,
> Separated from the sea, so near and yet so far,
> The mother country of which I once dreamed and read,
> *   *   *
> When the country falls in slumber, it's sick, weak;
> When its ill and shame will fall on it,
> Its people are so many, the land so huge,
> Mother country, just howl!
> Mother country, just howl!
> *   *   *
> When it was defeated, they sent us to the nursery
> And asked us to pay for the crime,
> A crime which, though we share as a country,
>   we can't address;
> Does a country, too, feel shame?[5]

Along with Wu Yung-fu, Chang Tung-fang, Lung Ying-chung (also a brilliant short story writer), and a group of poets from the Salt Flats in the Tainan area, together formed during World War II a core of Chinese consciousness.

However, we must bear in mind that, despite the opposition many Taiwanese poets held toward Japanese governance, such an attitude does not necessarily mean the same poets claimed a literary linkage to the Chinese mainland. For many years, local Taiwanese writers thought themselves "orphans" victimized both by foreign powers and by their own mother China. At one point, a local Taiwanese consciousness insisted upon the use of the Taiwanese dialect as a language of expression. In addition, as early as 1924, a local critic named Lien Wen-ch'ing wrote two articles for the October issue of the *The Taiwan People's News*—"The Social Nature of Language" and "The Future of Taiwanese Dialect"—which advocated the research and preservation of the Taiwanese dialect.[6]

Also, in 1929 the honorable historian Lien Ya-t'ang published articles in the November issue of *The Taiwan People's News* titled "The Responsibility of Organizing Taiwanese Dialect" and "The Initial Outcome of Organizing Taiwanese Dialect."[7] For many years, Lien Ya-t'ang himself had engaged in the study of the Taiwanese dialect; his edition of the four volumes of the *Taiwanese Dictionary* pioneered efforts to bring the study of Taiwanese to fruition.

We may judge these efforts of the two Liens as the outcome of national sentiments they had during the Japanese annexation, during which the oppressors strained to erase their subjects' identity. In 1930, Huang Shih-hui said in his article, "Why Not Promote Native Literature,"

> You are a Taiwanese. Above your head is the Taiwan sky. Below your feet is the Taiwanese earth. You see and hear in Taiwan, and the time you go through is a Taiwan experience. You speak the language of Taiwan. This is why you have to write in Taiwanese literature.[8]

Huang insisted that "writers should adopt the Taiwanese language to write prose, poetry, fiction, and ballads in order to describe things in Taiwan." He further explained that the Chinese written language, be it classical or modern vernacular, belongs to the elite, and that not all Taiwanese of lower social strata could fully understand it. Therefore, to create a literature for the masses, there was needed a native literature based on the adoption of the Taiwanese language.[9] With an attitude similar to Huang's, Kuo Ch'iu-sheng advocated a Taiwanese vernacular language to replace Chinese and Japanese. Kuo insisted that, because writing and speaking systems in Chinese and Japanese differ, the sameness of the written and spoken Taiwanese should make it a better language.[10]

Both Huang's and Kuo's views immediately met response, both pro and con. The opposition, however, was not all immediate. The Liens' promotion of a native literature written in Taiwanese dialect, for example, directly contrasted with Chang Wo-chung's concerns stated in 1925. In "The Meaning of the New Literature Movement," he coins two slogans: "The construction of new literature," and "the reformation of the Taiwanese language." In other words, Chang's mission was to elevate the Taiwanese dialect to more meaningfully express Mandarin Chinese; consequently, he thought, the construction of a new literature in Taiwan should not drift from the mainstream of new literature in China.[11]

It is evident that the background of the development of modern Chinese poetry in Taiwan is quite complicated. Poets bearing a strong Chinese sentiment were writing in Japanese; other poets, strongly committed to the Taiwanese identity, were writing in Japanese and Chinese. Generally speaking, after the 1937 ban on the use of Chinese, Taiwanese poets fell into a language vacuum, despite the 1945 recovery of Taiwan, and they have not yet fully recovered from this Chinese language deficiency.

Shortly after 1945, the Taiwanese eagerness to learn Mandarin and the Republican government's promotion of the Chinese language were positive signs of a Chinese revival. It should be noted that during this time there were some brilliant writers. One was Chung Li-ho, who, despite his consumptive ill health and deficiency in the Chinese language, continued up to his death in 1960 to produce brilliant, realistic short stories treating his native Taiwanese environment.[12] Other writers, however, like Wu Cho-liu and Yang Kuei, wrote just as tenaciously during the Japanese occupation, but would not have published had the island not been returned to the Chinese. Wu wrote the famous full-length novel, *The Orphan of Asia,* and Yang wrote a short story, "The Marriage of Mother Goose."[13] In the genre of poetry there existed poets like Wu Ying-t'ao and Lin Heng-t'ai, who were almost bilingual in Chinese and Japanese. Both were active with other poetry groups after the Republican government moved in 1949 from the mainland to the island.

Thus we begin to see forming a modern poetic tradition resulting from the combined efforts of local Chinese poets in Taiwan and mainland Chinese poets bringing to the island their own poetic traditions.

The foremost mainland Chinese poet, Chi Hsien, brought to the island his affinity for French symbolism and Chinese modernism. He had been associated with the modernists in Shanghai, who were influenced by the French symbolists Rimbaud and Baudelaire.[14] Before moving to Taiwan, Chi had been chief editor of two short-lived poetry journals in Shanghai, *Poetic Boundary* and *Heresy*, in 1944 and 1948 respectively. And, on February 1, 1953, Chi began to publish *Modern Poetry*, which was first intended as a monthly but after a few issues became a quarterly publication.[15] This journal soon became an arena for various poetic participants. Chi Hsien himself, Fang Ssu, Cheng Ch'ou-yu, Li Sha, Wu Ying-t'ao, Yung Tzu, Lo Men, Yang Huan, Hsin Yu, and P'eng Pang-chen were the most active; others contributed regularly, like Ya Hsien, Lin Ling, Chou Meng-tieh, Lin Heng-t'ai, Pai Ch'iu, Lo Fu, and Lo Ma (who later changed his name to Shang Ch'in). Among these names we find Wu Ying-t'ao, Lin Heng-t'ai, and Pai Ch'iu, local Taiwanese poets who merged with the mainlanders in a joint poetic effort. Their backgrounds were diverse: Chi Hsien was a high school teacher; Fang Ssu worked for the Central Library; Cheng Ch'ou-yu worked for the Port Authority in Keelung; Li Sha was a clerk in the Supreme Court; Yung Tzu worked in the Taipei Telecommunications Office, and later married Lo Men, who worked for the Civil Aeronautics Administration. Others, like Ya Hsien, Lo Fu, Hsin Yu, and P'eng Pang-chen, served in the military before being dispersed many years later to other, professional careers. And the group was not without its tragedies, like the death of Yang Huan, a poet of only twenty-four years who died when rushing through a railroad crossing to see a movie. All in all, we see gathering an historical group of talents from all walks of life devoting themselves unselfishly to the search for and promotion of a new Taiwanese poetry.

On February 1, 1956, with the thirteenth issue of *Modern Poetry*, there was published a proclamation of the formation of the Modernist School. Eighty-three names appeared on the list. In addition, an outspoken "modernist manifesto" voiced by Chi Hsien appeared, of which the following six tenets are excerpted:

1. We are a group of Modernists who select and express the spiritual elements of all new poetic schools since Baudelaire.

2. We regard new poetry in China as a horizontal transplant rather than a vertical succession. This is an overall view, a basic starting point, applying to both theory and practice.

3. We regard poetry as the exploration of a new continent, pioneering in a virgin island the expression of a new content, the creation of a new form, the discovery of new tools, the invention of new techniques.

4. We emphasize sensibility.

5. We pursue the purity of poetry.

6. We are patriotic, anticommunist, and support freedom and democracy.[16]

When it first retreated to Taiwan in 1949, the Republic soon realized that the literary policy in the mainland had proven vulnerable to the influence of leftist writings. The half-defunct government was most eager to search for a new literary model. Under these circumstances, turning to a powerful western model, congenial both in political ideology and intellectual content, was not only acceptable but inevitable. Moreover, establishing a Defense Treaty with the United States, and having closer commercial ties and a more extensive cultural exchange, prompted a desire to follow closely the most current literary phenomena of the west.

The emphasis on a more sophisticated language and themes, however, was reinforced by the progress of industrialization; in effect, this caused frustration and disillusionment with traditional values, particularly in rural areas. Therefore, the practice of the Modernists reflects an unsettled mind caught in the complexities of change, and suffering from a forced wish for escapism. Consider, for example, Chi Hsien's poems' which bear a true reflection of the alienated self. For many years in Taiwan, Chi established his trademark in poetic circles: pipe in mouth, walking stick in hand, and with the tallness of a betel palm tree:

I: A Betel Palm Tree

In the moon,
I stood,
Tall,
Like a betel palm tree.

When the wind came,
I made a noise:
Soughing, soughing,
Sough, sough, sough.[17]

In another poem entitled "Lonely Walk of a Wolf," he describes himself as follows:

I am a lone wolf in the wilderness.

Not a prophet,
Without even a sigh.

But with a few sharp shrieking howls,
I shake the hollow universe,
Making it tremble as if in malaria,
And the cold breeze it creates turns me quivering;
Such force,
Such joy![18]

These lines represent Chi's genuine effort to bring poetry to a clear flowing of the poetic consciousness. In fact, the poems from which the lines were taken have a much better effect than Chi's other type of western-oriented poetry, such as "S'en aller" or "The Death of Aphrodite." Thus, with Chi's undisputed leadership, we see a positive side of the "horizontal transplant" from which a pure, condensed poetic language is derived, independent of the May Fourth tradition in mainland China. While the mainland poets struggled to create a new poetic language in the 1930s and 1940s, they never went beyond a crude, artificial stage. By the time of this poetry, however, experimentation with various forms of poetic expression in Taiwan had brought the modern poets to a new realization: their pursuit was for an expression to visualize the poems of the mind.

On the other hand, we see a tremendous effort by local Taiwanese poets to merge with the mainstream. As mentioned above, owing to their slow adaptability to the Chinese language, they diverted the attention to diction by vehemently using the concreteness of form. Consider, for example, this poem from Lin Heng-t'ai:

Scenery

I.

By the side of
    the farm produce, there is
        farm produce, by the side of
the farm produce, there is
        farm produce, there is

Sunshine, sunshine, making long ears,
Sunshine, sunshine, long necks.

II.

Outside the windbreak
    there is windbreak
Outside the windbreak
    there is windbreak.
Outside the windbreak.

Then it's the sea, and the arrangement of waves,
The sea, and the arrangement of waves.[19]

Unlike the American Concretist principle, in which a concrete poem is based on the "concentration upon the physical material from which a poem or text is made,"[20] Lin's graphic images are more concerned with the overlapping of poetic contents producing a poetic image. Thus, we find that in his poems diction does not create pictures for the mind so much as the words' meanings lead to the perception of pictures.

The establishment of the *Blue Star* poetry society in 1954 was almost a "reactionary" movement against Chi Hsien's modernist practices. Yu Kuang-chung, one of the five founders of the society (with Ch'in Tzu-hao, Chung Ting-wen, Hsia Ch'ing, and Teng Yu-p'ing) recalled:

> Right in the beginning, we have acquiesced in that we want to organize an unorganized poetry society. Based on this cognition, we have not elected any president, nor have an agenda, nor proclaim any "ism." In general, our gathering is "reactionary" to Chi Hsien. Chi wanted to transplant western modern poetry to Chinese soil; we object. We have never taken the responsibility for carrying on the tradition of Chinese poetry, so do we arbitrarily need a "horizontal transplant"? Chi Hsien wants to expel lyricism, and to use cognition as a basic principle of creativity. Our style inclines toward the lyrical. Chi Hsien wants to banish rhymes and to use prose as a tool for poetry. Upon this point, our reaction is not unified . . .[21]

Though the opposition of the Blue Star poets was primarily against Chi Hsien, and though he played a dominant role with his leadership and personality, we must point out that he alone could not represent Modernists as a whole. The ultimate purpose in the formation of the Blue Star seems, then, to have been more of an "anti-Chi Hsien" act than an anti-Modernist one. This is particularly true with Ch'in Tzu-hao, whose defiance of Chi Hsien's leadership was not purely a matter of splitting from his poetic practices. Furthermore, although the Blue Star poets aimed at the perfection of lyrical poetry, while retaining their Chinese identity, Ch'in Tzu-hao's poems are actually more abstract and nihilistic than are his contemporaries', and thus represent another strain of modernist poetry not associated with Chi Hsien in practice. In addition, in light of the practices of modernist poets other than Chi Hsien, it is evident that several played pioneering roles in bringing modern poetry to its Taiwanese frontier. Fang Ssu's scintillating verses in the 1950s, such as "The Harp and the Flute" or "Nocturne," will forever be remembered as marking milestones in the country's poetic development, and we are saddened that Fang gave up writing soon after leaving for the United States in 1958. He resumed writing poetry in 1980, but has been unable to recapture the glorious moments of his early work.

From 1954 to 1964, the Blue Star movement produced a core of poets who form the lyrical mainstream of modern Chinese poetry. Yu Kuang-chung's resilience and facility in moving in and out of the classical and modern, the west and east; the legendary book vender Chou Meng-tieh's zen-buddhist poetry; Yeh Shan's soft touch of classical lyricism; and Lo Men's tragic consciousness, his often narrative but dramatic manner—all of them are characterized by a lyrical intensity created, on the one hand, by a perfect dexterity with language usage, and on the other, by a precision with poetic imagery. Among other consistently lyrical poets are Hsiang Ming, Yuan Nang, Huang Yung, Chang Chien, and Hsiung Hung.

Blue Star contributed more than poetry to the modern Chinese tradition. First appearing as a weekly literary supplement in the *Kung Lun News* was the *Blue Star Weekly*, which carried on for more than two hundred issues before ceasing publication in October 1958. There was, in addition, the *Blue Star Poetry Selections*, published as a quarterly, and at the close of 1958, Hsia Ch'ing edited the *Blue Star Poetry Broadside*, which was highly popular with its Taiwan audience. During these years, Blue Star poets staunchly defended modern poetry in Taiwan, often against venomous attacks launched by traditionalists and pedantic scholars. Despite the numerous polemics and controversies, the poets stood firm. They organized three poetry recitations, the last in 1964, at which the turnout of more than five hundred constituted a rare phenomenon in the early years of modern poetry in Taiwan.

In October 1954, the same year as the Blue Star's formation in Taipei, in southern Taiwan three navy officers—Ya Hsien, Lo Fu, and Chang Mo—gathered to form the Epoch poetry society. The first issue of *The Epoch* advocated a "national poetic form" which aimed at neither rational nor emotional narratives, but focused on the presentation of images and the development of poetic tension. However, the Epoch poets did not consolidate their style until 1959, when they expanded their journal to include not only poems but also criticism, as well as translations of western poetics.

In a way, we may see a linkage of the Epoch poets with the Modernists, not simply because there are poets who actually travel from one camp to the other, but because the Epoch's emphasis upon pure sensibility and the disavowal of lyrical styles is in line with Modernist practices. Special issues treating Paul Valéry, Rainer Maria Rilke, T. S. Eliot, and other western European poets and poetics have reflected the interests and practices of some Epoch poets who seek to create an illusionistic state of mind, as well as to present in their poems concrete, pictorial images. Furthermore, the initiation of automatic writing, of surrealism, and of symbolism, along with the introduction of the so-called "pure experience" apart from the interference of the intellect, had prompted some of the poets to engage in nihilism and unnecessary ambiguity. However, as pointed out by Chang Mo, a founder of the Epoch society, the success of such practices depend upon an individual's talent; the society associated with the poet cannot be assigned any blame.[22] The Epoch and surrealist poet, Shang Ch'in, for example, has successfully maintained with his spontaneous, conscious flow of the mind the rhythmic expression of automatic writing. His famous poems, such as "The Unbraided Queue," "The Giraffe," and "Faraway Lullaby" confirm Chang Mo's point.[23]

While trying to balance these three poetic powers as if they were the three kingdoms in ancient China, we must bear in mind that poetry societies are not political entities, and literary proclamations do not stand as ideologies. Literary giants may tend toward tyranny, as they have much influence, but seldom do they have full control over fellow poets or an audience. It is evident that these three poetry societies occupied a dominant position in Taiwanese poetry for more than twenty years (the *Epoch*, being the most long-lived journal, now enters its thirtieth year, but with a cast of young poets as editors). The dominance is obvious, even though the Modernists dispersed by 1963, much earlier than Chi

Hsien's retirement in 1976 to San Francisco.[24] The Blue Star Poetry Society ceased publication of its journal in 1964, and revived it only intermittently ten years later. However, in 1984, issues of *Blue Star* again appeared, this time in the firm and positive hands of an old associate, Hsiang Ming. The Epoch Poetry Society, with many of its leading members involved in the military and thus a stabilizing influence on the group in Taiwan, has consistently kept up its quarterly publication, with relatively few and brief interruptions.

All in all, these poetry societies should be regarded as a group rather than as separate entities, though their respective beliefs and styles differ. Individual poets too should be thought of more as belonging to the development of modern poetry as a whole in Taiwan, rather than as merely the affiliates of differing societies with their various tenets and proclamations. Lo Men, for example, was a member of and actively involved in all three societies. Also, such major poets of the Epoch group as Shang Ch'in, Hsin Yu, Yang Ling-yeh, and others, were once active Modernists. Even the *Li* (Bamboo Hat) poetry society, founded in 1964 with a cast of local Taiwanese poets, had representatives who had once been Modernists. It is evident that separating poets according to their involvement in various societies provides an inaccurate picture of the development of contemporary Chinese poetry in Taiwan.

Critics in Taiwan used to consider the year 1977 as the beginning of the Native Literature *(hsiang-t'u wen-hsueh)* controversy, in which writers began to show a strong social consciousness and a strong attachment to realism. It is interesting to note, though, that while Taiwan in the 1960s was heavily involved in modernism, especially in a poetry illustrating its authors' search for a new poetic diction, young poets of the 1970s were more interested in providing realistic content. In Taiwan, a concern for and eagerness to affirm their native reality prompted poets to challenge the practices of senior poets who had built a modernist tradition of individual feelings and symbolic expression. In answer to this challenge, Chi Hsien insisted in an editorial in 1957 that:

What modern poets are in search of is to create a pure, transcendent, and independent world. There is no such thing as "connotation," there is no need for "interpretation." If it were poetry, real poetry, it would have something tasteful and soothing, transparent and far-reaching about it. Only high intellectual minds come into unison and can attain a high spiritual joy, unspeakable and unsurpassable. Poetry is a literature of the elite, not for the masses. It is kind of art, not for practical use.[25]

The *Blue Star* also defended the ambiguity in modern poetry, as follows:

Modern poetry always circles around a subject without really pointing out what it is in the end. This is no trick, but a unique feature of modern poetry. It uses empty images to build up an elusive pagoda. Outside, it looks transparent and spotless, but no one knows which buddha is being worshipped inside. The highest realm of poetry is perhaps emptiness.[26]

Backed by such statements and some of the surrealist credos, modern poets have pushed themselves further and further into a position of nihilism as a means of escape from reality. In response to this tendency, T'ang Wen-piao, a literary critic and professor of mathematics by trade, wrote a series of articles in the early 1970s which stirred up what Yen Yuan-shu labeled "The case of T'ang Wen-piao."[27] Of the four articles written by T'ang in 1973—"Modern Poetry is Long Dead," "Sunset Time—A Preface for *Far Beyond the Plain*," "The Decadence of Poetry," and "What Time? What Place? What People?"[28]—the last two articles are the most controversial. In them, the author advocates the priority of a social function in poetry, and states that literature has to serve the masses rather than desert them. In "The Decadence of Poetry," T'ang lashes relentlessly at the decadence of the "art for art's sake" doctrine, and at the escapism from reality found in modern Taiwanese literature. He criticizes not only personal escapism but also escapism in word play, in the lack of ideology, and in the extensive submersion in lyricism. In "What Time? What Place? What People?" he even points out the problems with three major poets, Ch'ou Meng-tieh, Yu Kuang-chung, and Yeh Shan, and notes their misuse of the classical tradition in modern poetry. Ch'ou meng-tieh, according to T'ang, was the "solidification of classical poetry" because he brought in classical allusions of sadness and sorrow in his poetry. In addition, his sudden enlightenment was not genuinely buddhistic, because he was more concerned with relieving his own spiritual self than with putting himself in the larger context of wishing to save mankind. Yeh Shan is the "gasification of classical poetry" because his poems were passive, egotistical, sentimental, fragmentary, and beauty-oriented. Lastly, Yu Kuang-chung was the "liquefication of classical poetry" because he saw and adapted to only the decadent, worn-out imagery of classical Chinese poetry.

In retrospect, T'ang Wen-piao's criticism is more destructive than constructive in assessing the contribution of modern poets in Taiwan. His critical viewpoints are subjective, sometimes without context, and highly instigative. His criticiscm can hardly be called socialistic, though he does possess a strong social mentality and endorses a simpler, more realistic depiction of life, rather than the stationing of life on a complex, sophisticated plane. T'ang is, nonetheless, an intruder, one who has not participated in the painful process of creation and experimentation in the development of modern Chinese poetry as it rose from the dilapidation and ruins of the May Fourth tradition. Though his intentions may be good-natured and his acerbity ultimately harmless, his critical objectivity is questionable. Most serious of all, T'ang seems to have allied himself with the camp of the *Literature Quarterly,* which strongly advocates a literature for the people, and treats more protectively and kindly the novelists and poets of this school. Whereas he remains silent about some of the latter's truly second-rate works, he was exploded his sound and fury against the modernist poets.

On the other hand, T'ang Wen-piao's intrusion was beneficial in that it shocked a large group of confused readers in Taiwan who had become lost in a stream of surrealistic modernism. T'ang's message was a dose of strong medicine for these, allowing a sick and pale literary society to revive itself. The practices of modernists and surrealists had become so extreme that their poetic incantations were no more than indulgence in a self-ish romanticism. In addition, most of these poets, ironically not the ones T'ang Wen-piao criticized, possessed egos so inflated that they believed history would eventually vindicate them, and whatever they wrote would ultimately be honored as milestones in the development of literature. Numerous anthologies were published in these years, edited by poets who had befriended other poets. The expansion of this modernist mentality had become so monstrous that even literary scholars tended to sanctify this school in articles with perspectives ranging from new critical to structuralist. T'ang Wen-piao's timely criticism appropriately helped quell this unfortunate situation.

In 1972, Kuan Chieh-ming (John Kwan Terry), an English professor at the National University of Singapore, came across a volume of English translations of modern Taiwanese poetry. He and one of his graduate students read the volume, and both felt that these poems, though admittedly in translation, actually sounded more like they had been composed in English than in Chinese. Kuan wrote two articles, "The Dilemma of Modern Chinese Poetry" and "The Illusion of Modern Chinese Poetry," both of which were published in the literary supplement of *China Times,*[29] a leading newspaper on the island of Taiwan with a circulation of over one million. The appearance of these articles in *China Times* was no accident. Kao Hsin-chiang, poet and chief editor of the supplement, was the major force behind the scene; he wanted to bring Kuan's articles to the attention of the large and varied literary audience on the island. Kuan's point was very simple. He merely wished to show how unwise modern Taiwanese poets had been to give up their Chinese tradition, on the one hand, and to become imitators of Western poetry on the other. Upon the appearance of Kuan's second article in September of 1972, T'ang Wen-piao had already returned to Taiwan and was teaching as a visiting professor of mathematics at National Taiwan University. He immediately responded to Kuan with the article, "Let's First Review Ourselves."[30] Both T'ang's and Kuan's articles drew immediate attention and created vehement discussions. At last, Taiwanese poets and their audience were taking into account the need for a countermodernist trend in modern Chinese poetry.

The year 1971 saw the beginning of the poetry society *Lung Tsu* (Dragons), which included such members as Kao Shang-ch'in (pseudonym for Kao Hsin-chiang), Lin Fu-erh (poet, publisher at Lin-pai Publishers, and now editor of the *Taiwan Poetry Quarterly*), Hsin Mu, Lin Huan-chang, Chiao Lin, and others. In 1972, after the appearance of Kuan Chieh-ming's articles mentioned earlier, the Dragons published a special issue on poetry criticism. Both T'ang and Kuan had articles printed in this issue, and both articles again created quite a stir.[31] Nevertheless, the publication of this special issue was a turning point in modern poetry in Taiwan; for one reason, there was the harsh criticism from T'ang and Kuan, and for another, Yu Kuang-chung's article calling for a change in modernism softened its tone.[32] There was in this issue, however, an overwhelming consensus that Chinese poetry needed a national character, and that to be truly Chinese required one to look back to his origins and begin to grow from his roots. The urge for a national character became the slogan of the Dragon poets: "We bang our gongs, beat our drums, and play our dragon dance." In a prefatory remark to the special issue, Kao Shang-ch'in wrote:

> Examined under scrutiny, many modern poets in Taiwan appear to have gradually drifted away from tradition and society in the last twenty years of modern poetry as it has progressed along the roads of art. In these poets' solitary contemplation and deliberate creation, they seem to have forgotten that they are still living among people, and that their poems still belong to the people. They are too fond of their own works, and the literal meaning of their work. . . . In addition, with the wholesale adoption of foreign thought, vocabulary, and creative theories, they have confused themselves in time and space. In other words, they have lost the soil for their own roots.[33]

All this discussion about the search for a nationalistic, native, and realistic literature laid the foundation for the arrival in 1977 of the Native Literature. In the ten-year period from 1970 to 1980, more than twenty poetry societies actively promoted modern poetry in Taiwan. Aside from the aforementioned *Dragons* and older poetry societies of *Epoch, Blue Star, Li,* and the *Vineyard,* there were the *Mainstream, Tempest, Lamp Worship, Great Earth, Back Waves, Wind Lanterns, May Be, Poets, Grass Roots, Messages, Lupus, Great Ocean, Green Land, Small Grass, Corridor, Poetic Trace, Eight Palm Brooks, Grand Master,* and *Sunlight Ensemble.* Some did not last long enough to make a marked impression on the poetic world; however, it would be unfair to assume that only big-name poets make poetry groups famous. The contributions and efforts of young poets should be evaluated from a historical perspective. Indeed, with the active and unselfish promotion of modern poetry by many young poets, poetic activities in Taiwan took a major shift in direction, one quite different from the practices of the senior poets. There was a strong sense of "belonging" to the island and a reconciliation of the individual with the masses. Literary supplements in newspapers began to take modern poetry seriously, treating it as an indispensable genre and regularly publishing it. Because they used a more lucid manner of expression, young poets were more acceptable to the general public than the older poets, some of whom had been a virtual nightmare for editors and readers alike.

On the other hand, senior poets have undergone great changes in both their poetic styles and content. With the test of time, many have faded from the scene, perhaps because of a lack of creativity. Others linger on, but their poems more or less repeat earlier works. In the span of the last twenty years, the most consistent poets have been Yu Kuang-chung, Yang Mu, and Lo Fu. It is interesting to note that, while all are Chinese poets, each has lived elsewhere during the last decade. Yu has been in Hong Kong, Yang in Seattle, and Lo in Taipei. Of the three, Yu is the most prolific, is capable of using a large variety of forms, and can vary his content. He once commented on his own poetic creativity:

> In old China, there was once a story of a writer who ran out of ideas. In fact, modern poets seem to have run out of ideas more quickly than classical ones. I feel that the talent of a writer lies in his sensitivity to life and expression. What we term "out of ideas" is the condition of being no longer sensitive to life, and

thus running out of things to write. Or, he is no longer sensitive to expression, and his poetic forms become stiff. People used to think the talent of a poet lies in his expression and form, but they seldom know that it takes more talent and learning to explore new subjects and new themes. . . . My choice of subjects is not wide enough but I am not in danger of drying up. I believe that a sensitive person will always have something to say, if he still loves others, if he still loves nature, and his national civilization and tradition. I even feel that a poet should tire more easily of his existing subject matter than his readers. In doing so, he can walk ahead and lead his readers in search of new forms and content.[34]

Yu admits that his ambition has always been to search for a rich variety of subject matter, and thus his style frequently changes. In recent years, his classical touch has still captured thousands of Chinese readers, but his style apparently has undergone changes to produce a more lucid message. In a poem entitled, "Lord, Do Not Cross the River," we have a demonstration of Yu's typical combination of classical and modern:

Lord, do not cross the river, a barbed wire stretches out its hand.
Lord, you did cross the river, a telescope aims at you,
You fell into the river and died, a barrage of bullets whistling
    through you,
What could I do with you, Lord,
A bunch of white reeds shaking their heads.

A flash of the searchlight cautioning:
Lord, do not cross the river,
A water patrol boat howling,
Lord, you did cross the river,
A flock of sharks rushing in,
You fell into the river and died,
A pool of blood gushing above water,
Even my song is useless.[35]

This poem is a combination of the classical *yueh fu* poem "K'ung-hou Harp Tune," written around the third century A.D. According to the legend:

Ts'ui-pao in *Ku chin chu* says, "As far as the 'K'ung-hou Harp Tune' is concerned, it was the creation of Li Yu, the wife of Ho-li Tzu-kao, who was a guard in Korea. Tzu-kao got up one morning to pole his boat. A grey-haired, deranged person with his long hair let down, was carrying a gourd-shaped container. He tried to wade across the river, against the current. His wife followed him, trying to stop him, but to no avail. He was drowned in the river as a result. Then, the wife took a K'ung-hou harp and sang:

Lord, do not cross the river,
Lord, you did cross the river,
You fell into the river and died?
What could I do with you, Lord?

The tune was quite pathetic, and at the end of the song, she also committed suicide by drowning herself. Tzu-kao went home and told Li Yu about the incident. Li Yu was so moved by it that she wrote down its tune to the accompaniment of the K'ung-hou harp. Those who heard the song shed tears without exception. Li Yu taught her neighbor, Li Jong, the tune and named it "The K'ung-hou Harp Tune."[36]

For the first half of the first stanza, Yu Kuang-chung has used the classical poem; he uses its lines again in the second stanze, interspersing among the lines the description of a tragic incident involving mainland and Chinese refugees who tried to swim across the border waters to Hong Kong. Thus, the theme of the poem addresses the tragedy of those many who did not make the journey successfully. They were either caught by the Hong Kong government patrol boats or were eaten by sharks. The poem is well contrived because it combines a tragic past and present. Like "montages" used in movies, the poem superimposes images of the historical over the modern tragedy. The stubbornness of the grey-haired, deranged person trying to cross the river equals the craziness of refugees risking their lives for freedom. Both are doomed, and the sense of the old man's, as well as his wife's, helplessness appears in both the classical song and the poet's rendition.

Unlike Yu Kuang-chung's fondness for self-metamorphosizing, Yang Mu's consistent pursuit is the condensation of image and metaphor. He is, thus, a poet who insists "against interpretation." Poetry is something to be felt instead of told. Nevertheless, he is no nihilist, although his conscious ego has often driven him to react ultrasensitively to his environment. In his recent "Interchange" columns in the *United Daily* he has expressed sharp critical views on the social and political problems in Taiwan and overseas. Still, his lyrical voice remains one of the foremost and best in modern Chinese poetry today. Part of "Snow of Yesterday: A Song" appropriately conveys his intense feelings about and keen observations of nature:

> Yesterday, when it came down to the middle of the mountain,
> That snowline (on a dark, gloomy afternoon), I felt
> Had already approached me,
> And I kept sinking;
> There was a flying whiteness falling on
> The dark greenish tips of the pine forest;
> It was a guiding,
> A passion of the universe.
> Yesterday, when for the first time since winter
> The snowline finally dropped to the mountain's middle,
> We had a hunch
> That it would maintain its heavy acceleration.
> Maybe without my being conscious of what happened,
> It quickly slid to the Lutheran church tops, by the slope,
> And then quietly fell
> Finally on our window;
> When I also fell back into the present.
> Even the walls were piled with white snow,
> It fell to touch upon the positions of nearly zero at sea level;
> Back by the porch
> Were some hesitant prints;
> Now, from a squirrel, I suspect,
> Or two, visiting us when we were out,
> And then left.
> All the road exits are closed,
> People rest in their houses;
> It's good that their basements are stored with sufficient food and
>   wine;

They wake up in bed and drink soup,
Sit before the fireplace, listen to weather broadcasts,
Take their baths and go to bed;
Snow keeps happily falling,
It's nice that Vitamin C and birth-control pills are in the closet;
Snow keeps happily falling,
Has already dropped below the linen sheets,
Lower than our shoulders—it keeps
Falling happily. . . .[37]

While established poets remain working in a "tug-o-war with eternity," to quote Yu Kuang-chung, younger poets try to work on more simplified structures with less complicated schemes and fewer symbolic implications. They head into two major directions. One is the use of short lyrics, in a single poem's aim at a single message. For example, Lin Huan-chang's volume of poetry called *Trees by the Highway* contains a series of poems using trees by the highway as personae:

When the rain starts to fall,
There is not much of a feeling.
Now, a lonely me
All by myself
Standing by the roadside,
I feel that
I have too little to wear
Like poor people.
But winter is just starting,
Days are long.
                    "Poor People"[38]

We by the side of the road,
With no one to care.

We were born without knowing
What sorrow is,
Then we were transplanted
To a destined place to grow,
No words, no sound.

> Wordlessly, we bear
> The lonely years,
> We keep bearing.
>   "No One to Care"[39]

Practicing these simplified messages may soon lead a poet to monotony; consequently, many poets turn to children's literature to be able to follow their practice. Lin Huan-chang now writes nothing but children's literature, including, of course, children's poems. Other young poets, like Li Nan, Su Shao-lien, and Chan Ch'e have experimented with writing children's verse, but although some of the poems are well designed and written, the overall result of their endeavors is not very fruitful.

A second direction young poets have taken is the use of loose sentence structures and everyday language in poetry. In the past, senior poets tried to develop a highly condensed syntax in poetry. They had created a highly technical and well developed poetic diction, and it surpassed that of the mainland poetry, which had ceased developing in this direction in the 1950s. On the other hand, the density of this language restricts the narrative function of poetry; thus describing people and events becomes difficult. Chan Ch'e, a young Taiwanese poet, has written an autobiographical poem entitled "Papa Came to See Me," in which he portrays the two generations of native Taiwanese:

> Twenty years ago, one autumn morning
> You came to East Taiwan empty-handed
> In the clamor of a confused morning market
> Some small rascals got hold of the market place
> In a scene where an old woman was intimidated
> You quickly threw away your bag
> And furiously picked up a carrying pole
> Indiscriminately, you beat up and dispersed both the cops and
>   the rascals
> You again ended up drifting. . . .

The poem continues, narrating not only the father's life, but in addition the relationship between father and son:

Last year, I took you to a movie
We both thought of that "Godfather,"
His shoulder and back are so thick and solid
What was he doing?
What for?
Papa,
You said you were not the American watching American
    movies
You said you didn't have American time to kill and make money
You said you were not Italian either
Italians allied with the Japanese and Germans
You said you've already suffered enough in Southeast Asia,
    fighting
You knew what they were doing
You said you were Chinese and Taiwanese
The kind of Taiwanese unafraid of cheaters or oppressors
Of trampling or corruption.[40]

In most of Chan Ch'e's poetry there is a sentimental tone regarding the suffering Taiwanese living through historical trage-dies. In his collection of poems called *Earth Please Speak Up*, he writes about the assassination of his great grandfather and the insults and torture suffered by his grandfather at the hands of the Japanese, in "Written for My Great Grandfather and My Grand-father." Two other poems, "She Is Not Mute" and "A Quick Glimpse of Ku Ling-lin," tell of a young prostitute named White Cloud, whose mother was forced by poverty to sell her daughter into that profession. Although White Cloud's mother is mute, White Cloud is not, and, drifting from one place to another, she ulti-mately meets the young poet and tells him her story. "Old Liu's Dawn" concerns a retired mainland soldier who has become a morning paper boy. As exemplifed with these, we see in Chan Ch'e's poetry a large variety of subjects not found in the works of established poets.

Whereas the poems of Chan Ch'e, Chiang Hsun, Shih Shan-chi, and other young poets were published in avant garde and political-intellectual journals such as *Hsiung Shih Art Monthly* and *Summer Wave*, the movement of Native Literature came to its most active stage when its advocates clashed with the right-wing traditionalists.[41] Among the poets emerging on the scene, Shih San-chih can be viewed as the epitome of a poet in transition. Starting out as a modernist, he was instantly endorsed by Yu Kuang-chung as one who would continue in the modernist tradition. Eventually, he joined the Dragons, and his viewpoint changed drastically. He himself admitted that after reading articles by T'ang Wen-piao, Kuan Chieh-ming and others, he wanted very much to abandon the path he had previously taken. His subject matter narrowed from selection among a large variety of topics to that of everyday events in Taiwanese society. In this way, Shih San-chih comes very close to Chiang Hsun and Chan Ch'e in style, as they are all characterized by the strong commitment to portray a social reality.[42]

But, as earlier mentioned, the use of everyday language does not guarantee strong poetic tension, and there are young poets who wish to compromise the complexity of modernism with the simplicity of realism. The establishment of *Grass Roots,* headed by Lo Ch'ing and others, proclaimed in 1975 its four major principles:

1. Being in an age when our country is split into two sides, we can't help but have a deep concern for our fate and for the reflection of our real situation.

2. Poetry is many-sided. So is life. We don't feel that poetry has to be a criticism of life, but should reflect life and, thus, truly reflect our nation.

3. We understand that popularizing and professionalizing poetry are the same thing. The difference depends on the treatment of the subject matter and the artistic treatment. We wish to see each side have its unique achievement, without being partial to either side.

4. We respect the past, but do not linger on it. We are anxious for the future, but confident in it. We embrace our tradition. but we don't repel the West. We wish to dedicate our united, zealous spirit to the land we now embrace: Taiwan.[43]

We now see for the first time a reconciliation between the new realists and the modernists. As the young poet and critic Hsiang Yang pointed out, the most important meaning of the Grass Roots proclamation lies in its forward vision and its desire to reorganize what the Dragons pursued in the early seventies, by combining a new aesthetics with the young poets' concern for a "national style," "reality," "respect for the vernacular," "emphasis on the native," and "multiconceptual" viewpoints.[44]

Most of the young poetry societies did not last long, and their respective journals folded with them. By 1979, the formation of the *Sunlight Ensemble* represented a regrouping of poets from more than nine societies. Headed by Hsiang Yang and others, the social consciousness of these poets rose steadily to a meaningful height, and has enabled them to extend their poetic sensibilities to achieve a greater understanding of human life. Above all, the most significant outcome of these experiences and endeavors is the recognition of a new lyric tradition, be it art for art's sake or art for life's sake. This tradition penetrates deeply into modern Chinese life, and leads the reader with its rippling, lyrical voices to a higher understanding of the contemporary Chinese mind.

Unfortunately, the *Sunlight Ensemble* was short-lived, disbanding in 1985. Again, the old poetry journals crept back to the poetic scene. *Epoch* was reorganized with younger poets as editors. *Li,* with its strong native consciousness, is still published regularly. The ups and downs of modern poetry in Taiwan are like the beginning poem of the *Romance of the Three Kingdoms,* in which the classical novelist, Lo Kuan-chung, writes:

> The Long River passes east away,
> Surge over surge,
> Whiteblooming waves sweep all heroes on
> As right and wrong, triumph and defeat all turn unreal.
> But ever the green hills stay
> To blush in the west-waning day.[45]

With the synopsis of the recent history of Taiwanese and Chinese poetry behind us, we may state the goal of this book: to scan and delineate the major poetic activities of the last twenty years. I have concentrated on poets and poetry of these last two decades to avoid repeating material published in other anthologies. One exception is Ya Hsien, who, although having written more than twenty years ago, I consider a foremost poet influential in articulating the current poetry scene. Another atypical poet, who ceased writing for some time and only recently resumed, is Cheng Ch'ou-yu. Because his previous works are more widely acclaimed, and thus well represented in other anthologies, I have selected material from his recent writings. Also, I believe that a poet's career, particularly a poet with consistent creative potential, should be viewed over a long stretch of time. Thus, I concentrate upon senior poets and the writings of Yang Mu, Yu Kuang-chung, and Lo Fu. Twenty years seems to be an appropriate span of time for the emergence of a poetic generation, or so thought T. S. Eliot, who stated the following in his first annual Yeats lecture delivered to the Friends of the Irish Academy at the Abbey Theatre, in Dublin:

> The generation of poetry in our age seems to cover a span of about twenty years. I do not mean that the best work of any poet is limited to twenty years: I mean that is about the length of time before a new school or style of poetry appears. By the time, that is to say, that a man is fifty, he has behind him a kind of poetry written by men of seventy, and before him another kind written by men of thirty.[46]

It is a cruel truth that editing an anthology is no easy task, particularly when the editor must double as translator, and bring to the project both linguistic ability and a flair for editorial discrimination. So is it true that translating an individual poetry volume is less taxing than translating and editing an anthology. The difficulty, however, lies not so much in the fact that a variety of poets' stylistic complexities are harder to handle than those of a single poet, but that the translating-editing process further requires a thorough understanding of a literary milieu, from its origins and roots in tradition to its contemporary character. In addition, I tend to focus more on the ontological meaning of the poems, and thus do not translate them on too literal a basis. I insist that translation is an understanding, particularly in poetry, not the literal rendition of words. Consequently, the ultimate purpose of my translations is to search for a western model, if possible, and at the same time not to lose the poems' original flavor. Such an attempt may fail in the rendition of classical Chinese poetry, but I have not encountered too much difficulty in rendering modern poems.

To dwell on the time and effort that went into this volume would be as superfluous as to insist on how judiciously the poets and poems have been chosen. On a highly selective basis, I have chosen thirty-two poets who I consider deserve a presentation of their works. I do know that more could have been included; however, I believe that all anthologies are subjective, and indeed ought to be. When conceived, begun, and completed, an anthology results in more unhappy than happy people. Those not selected think they should have been; those selected did not have enough, or the right, poems anthologized. (Chinese have an insatiable appetite for fame!) However the poems, and the number selected, were chosen for their quality, regardless of how many books their authors may have published. As the old saying goes, you can't please all of the people all of the time; thus, I have chosen to please my conscience and poetic judgment.

This book has undergone many phases of change before arriving at the form it now has. When in its first draft, Noriko Mizuta read and revised the manuscript for me, making various suggestions. During my earlier years at the University of Southern California, she was the only person to endorse with constant encouragement and confidence all my various writings, Chinese or English. Now that I am confident of myself, she has left. Dale Coleman copy edited the manuscript in its later stages, and his poetic sensibility has added to it an extra degree of stylistic sensibility.

Two other supporters were present throughout the volume's development. One who remains in my heart, and to whom I am indebted for his friendship and support, is Marshall Cohen, Dean of the School of Humanities at the University of Southern

California. In an era when humanistic endeavors have some difficulty finding support, those of us involved in those endeavors are more than pleased to find a voice in the administration who will plead our case—not that the case ever has been unreasonable, but because society occasionally becomes forgetful, just as the Taiwanese poets mentioned earlier somehow lost a sense of their nationalism. In those times, support is a lifeline, and I can only attribute it to a fortunate providence to have made Dean Cohen's acquaintance. In the same vein of gratitude, to Irwin Chet Lieb, then Vice President and Dean of the College of Letters, Arts and Sciences, I pay special tribute. His concern for the humanities is more than academic, more than professional: it is heartfelt. He supported me throughout this endeavor, and trusted the nature and scope of my project with a concern that surpassed mere interest in my professional goals. Without that trust and confidence, this volume would never have been brought through the various stages to its conclusion.

Dominic Cheung
University of Southern California

Notes

1. For more information on the controversy between Chang Wo-chun and Lian Ya-t'ang, see Wu Ying-t'ao's article, "A Retrospect of Taiwanese New Poetry," in *Reader's Guide to Modern Poetry*, 現代詩導讀, later cited as *RGMP*, ed. Chang Han-liang and Hsiao Hsiao, vol. 4: *Theory and Historical Reference* (Taipei: Ku-hsiang Publishing Co., 1979), p. 370.

For further detail, readers should also consult Ch'en Shao-t'ing's *A Brief History of the New Literature Movement in Taiwan* 台灣新文學運動簡史 (Taipei: Lien-ching Publishing Co., 1977), pp. 21–24. Later cited as *Brief History*.

2. Chang Kuang-chih, son of Chang Wo-chun, has a brief biography of his father in "Words from the Editor," in *Collected Works of Chang Wo-chun* 張我軍文集 (Taipei: Pure Literature Publishing Co., 1975), pp. 1–3.

3. Ibid., p. 37.

4. See Liang Ching-feng's "Afterword: An Island's Song" in *New Taiwanese Literature Under Japanese Occupation*, 日據下台灣新文學, vol. 4: *Poetry*, ed. Li Nan-Heng (Taipei: Ming-t'an Publishing Co., 1979), p. 426.

5. "Mother Country," by Wu Yung-fu, in *Brief History*, pp. 155–56.

6. Ibid., pp. 61–62.

7. Ibid., pp. 64–65.

8. Ibid., p. 66.

9. Ibid., pp. 67–68.

10. Ibid., pp. 69–70.

11. Ibid., p. 20.

12. For Chung Li-ho's life and his works, readers can consult *The Short Stories of Chung Li-ho*, 鍾理和短篇小說集 (Taipei: Ta-chiang Publishing Co., 1970), and *The Compendium of Chung Li-ho*, 8 vols., 鍾理和全集 (Taipei: Yuan-hsiang Publishing Co., 1976).

13. *Brief History*, p. 15. For a study of the nationalist movement during the Japanese occupation of Taiwan, readers can consult the *History of the Taiwanese National Movement*, 台灣民族運動史, by Yeh Yung-chung, et al. (Taipei: Tzu-li Evening News, 1971).

14. Hsu Shih-hsu's "Thirty Years of Modern Chinese Poetry" in the *United Daily News*. Taipei, June 3, 4, and 5, 1984. Hsu pointed out that Chi's modernist spirit continues the modernist tradition of Tai Wang-shu in Shanghai, who edited *Modern* (1932), *Modern Poetic Style* (1935), and *New Poetry* (1936).

15. Yang Mu, "About Chi Hsien's Modern Poetry Society and the Modernist School," in *RGMP*, vol. 4. p. 383.

16. See *A Compendium of Modern Chinese Literature (Poetry)*, 中國現代文學大系, prefaced

by Lo Fu (Taipei: Chu-jen Publishing Co., 1972), p. 4. For details of the tenets, see *RGMP*, vol. 4, pp. 387–88.

17. "A Betel Palm Tree," by Chi Hsien, in Chi Pi-hua's *Appreciation of Lyrics from Taiwan*, 台灣抒情詩賞析 (Hong Kong: Nan-yueh Publishing Co., 1983), p. 7.

18. Ibid., p. 8.

19. "Scenery," by Lin Heng-t'ai, in *Anthology of New Chinese Poetry*, 中國新詩選, ed. Lin Ming-teh (Taipei: Chang-an Publishing Co., 1980), pp. 229–30. For an analysis of these poems, see *RGMP*, vol. 1, pp. 63–66.

20. Mary Ellen Solt, "Introduction," *Concrete Poetry: A World View* (Bloomington, Indiana: Indiana University Press, 1969). I have quoted this line from X. J. Kennedy's *An Introduction To Poetry* (Boston: Little, Brown, 1974), p. 199.

21. Yu Kuang-chung, "The Seventieth Birthday," in *RGMP*, vol. 4, p. 395. In fact, Yu mentioned that the later coalition of Huang Yung, Yeh Shan, Lo Fu, and others was mainly for the purpose of opposing Ch'in Tzu-hao. Western languages are written or read horizontally, while Chinese languages are written or read vertically.

22. "A Free Talk on the Poetry Journal in These Thirty Years," by Chang Mo, *Epoch*, no. 62 (Taipei, 1983), p. 142. Even Ya Hsien himself denied that he was a surrealist. See "Introduction," *Compendium of Contemporary Chinese Literature* 當代中國新文學大系（詩）, (Taipei: T'ien-shih, 1980), pp. 10–11.

23. For an English translation of "Giraffe" and "The Unbraided Queue," see Wai-lim Yip's *Modern Chinese Poetry* (Iowa City, Iowa: University of Iowa, 1970), pp. 5–6.

24. Chi Hsien recently published a volume of poetry, *Late Years*, 晚景 (Taipei: Erh-ya Publishing Co., 1985). For his earlier works, readers can consult Hsian Ming's article, "The Forever Betel Palm Tree," in *Wen Hsun Bi-monthly*, no. 19, 文訊雙月刊 (1985), pp. 123–28.

25. Chi Hsien's editorial was written for his poetry journal *Modern Poetry*, no. 16 (1957), p. 2. I have quoted this passage from T'ang Wen-piao's *Heaven Is Not Ours*, 天國不是我們的 (Taipei: Lian-chin Publishing Co., 1976), p. 149.

26. See T'ang's *Heaven Is Not Ours*, p. 150. The passage came out in *Blue Stars*, no. 2 (1957), p. 5.

27. I am greatly appalled by poetry anthologies such as *China's Ten Great Poets*, 中國十大詩人選, ... etc.

28. T'ang Wen-piao, *Heaven Is Not Ours*.

29. Kuan's articles first appeared in the *China Times Literary Supplement*; I have quoted him from Chao Chih-t'i's *Literature, Don't Run*, 文學，休走 (Taipei: Yuan-hsing Publishing Co., 1976), pp. 137–44.

30. Chao Chih-t'i, *Literature, Don't Run*, pp. 193–200.

31. See the special issue of *Lung-Tsu Critical Issue on Poetry*, no. 9, 龍族評論專號 (1973), Taipei.

32. Yu Kuang-chung, "What to Change in Modern Poetry," 現代詩怎麼變, in ibid., pp. 10–13.

33. Kao Shang-ch'in, "In Search and In Retrospect," 探索與回顧, in ibid., p. 6.

34. See Yu Kuang-chung, *Selected Poems*, 余光中詩選 (Taipei: Hung Fan Bookstore, 1981), p. 6.

35. Ibid., p. 303.

36. I have adopted the legend and English translation from Ying-hsiung Chou's article, "'Lord, Do Not Cross the River': Literature as a Mediating Process," in *China and the West: Comparative Literature Studies*, ed. William Tay, et al. (Hong Kong: The Chinese University of Hong Kong, 1980), p. 112.

37. Yang Mu, "Snow of Yesterday: a Song," 昨天的雪的歌, in *Unitas*, no. 7, 聯合文學 (1985), Taipei, pp. 120–21.

38. Lin Huan-chang, *Trees by the Highway*, 公路邊的樹 (Taipei: Pu Ku Publishing Co., 1983), pp. 8–9.

39. Ibid., pp. 10–11.

40. Chan Ch'e, *Earth, Please Speak Up*, 土地請站起來說話, (Taipei: Yuan-liu Publishers, 1983), pp. 36–52.

41. Readers should consult Yu T'ien-ts'ung, ed., *Collection on the Native Literature Controversy*, 鄉土文學討論集 (Taipei: n.p., 1978). Representing views opposed to Native Literature is P'eng Ko's edition of *An Overall Criticism of Current Literary Controversy*, 當前文學問題總批評 (Taipei: Ch'ing-hsi New Literature Society, 1977).

42. See Hsu Nan-ts'un's (another pseudonym for novelist Ch'en Yin-chen) lengthy preface for *Selected Poems of Shih Shan-chi*, 施善繼詩選 (Taipei: Yuan-ching Publishers, 1981), pp. 7–63.

43. See Hsiang Yang's article, "Modern Poetry in the 1970's," 七十年代現代詩風潮試論, a monograph published in *Symposium of Modern Poetics*, 現代詩學研討會 (Taipei, 1984), pp. 59–60. The article was later collected in *Wen Hsun Bi-Monthly*, no. 12, (1984), pp. 47–76.

44. Ibid., p. 60.

45. I have used Moss Roberts' translation in *Three Kingdoms* (New York: Pantheon Books, 1976), p. 3.

46. T. S. Eliot, *On Poetry and Poets* (New York: Noonday, 1964), p. 295.

The isle is full of noises,
Sounds and sweet airs, that give delight, and hurt not.
Sometimes a thousand twangling instruments
Will hum about mine ears; and sometimes voices,
That, if I then had wak'd after long sleep,
Will make me sleep again.

—Shakespeare,
The Tempest, 3.2.146

Yang Mu (1940–   )

Yang Mu was a young college graduate from Tunghai University in central Taiwan when he emerged in the early 1960s as one of that decade's most promising poets. By the time he finished college, he had published two volumes of poetry under the pen name Yeh Shan. In 1972, upon receiving his doctorate in comparative literature from the University of California at Berkely, he changed his pen name to Yang Mu and began to teach at the University of Washington, in Seattle. He continues to publish as Yang Mu.

Yang Mu's poetry has remained creative and experimental over the years while many of his contemporaries have, one after another, faded into silence. Yang's poetry consistently exhibits sophisticated poetic ideas, often delivered in compressed images and ingenious metaphors. In 1978, he published the first volume of his *Collected Poems,* attempting to conclude his "Yeh Shan phase"; his poems, nevertheless, remain highly imaginative. Yang Mu is also an accomplished essayist. In recent years, particularly, he has paid more attention to critiquing and editing the work of established prose writers. His free-lance "Interchange" in the *United Daily* has attracted a diversified audience, encouraging him to deliver a social message to his readers. In addition, he is the Chinese translator of Garcia Lorca's *Romancero Gitano.*

Poetry:

At The Brink of the Water, 1963
The Flower Season, 1963
Lantern Boat, 1966
No Crossing, 1969

Let the Wind Recite

1.

If only I could write you a summer-poem,
When the reeds
Drastically multiply;
The sun leaps up to the waist
And flows divergently past the two legs;
When a new drum
Starts to crack, if only

I could write you an autumn-poem,
Swinging in a small boat,
Wetting twelve watermarks;
When sadness curls
Like a yellow dragon in the riverbed,
Letting the rushing mountain stream arise
From the wounded eyes splashing, if only

I could write you a winter-poem,
To witness finally the ice, the snow,
And a shrunken lake;
To witness someone's midnight visitation

To you, awake in a bed of hurried dreams—
When you were relocated in a faraway province,
Given a lantern, and asked
To sit with patience,
Without tearful eyes.

2.

If they won't allow you
To mourn or to weave
For springtime;
If they ask you
To sit quietly, to wait,
A thousand years later,
After spring passes,
Your name will remain, summer;
They will return you,
Take away your ring, your dress,
Cut your hair short
And leave you at my tolerant water's brink;
You will belong to me at last.

At last, you will belong to me,
To be bathed, to be given wine,
Peppermint candies, new dresses;
Your hair will grow again
To the length of former days;
Summer will remain your name.

3.

Then I will write you
A spring-poem, when all
Has regenerated—
So young and shy

To see one's own maturing shadow
In the water,
I will let your tears fall freely,
Will design new dresses for you,
Will make candles for your first night.

Then you will let me write on my bosom
A spring-poem;
Heartbeats will be the rhythms,
Blood, the rhymes,
Breasts will be the images,
And a mole, the metaphor.
I will lay you down on a warm lake,
And let the wind recite.

Wine Vessels: Two Labels

First Label: Clay (to Ya Hsien)

After he returned home, they said
He neither drinks, nor smokes,
Nor becomes too poetic;
What remains, finally and lovely
Hung on the western sky
Is an evening in which to stroll with his woman.
Leaves, starlight, and running water all agree,
No more quarrels, this summer.

As for birds and fishes,
Once the moon rises, forget them!
This Japanese wine vessel
Sticks out its rotund belly,
To bear the true void.

Every time I hold the handle 45 degrees
And slantingly point to the Little Bear,
My drinking does not lack
The interest of astrology,
Or you may call it mathematics.

Second Label: Porcelain (to Ch'ou-yu)

沢の鶴 comes from the border city,[1]
の is pronounced *no,*
The consonant of *nu* added to the vowel of *ko.*
No means *chih,* or "of."
The upright position of the white porcelain reveals
A tinge of floating cloud across the neck,
Gradually, I am filled with intoxication,
Day and night.

"Those who seek wine
Never shun adventure . . ."
Across the mountain and the river,
Sawa no tsuru.[2]

Villagers fetching water wait by the well,
Charcoal fires burn under the rain shelter,
A copy editor coughs,
A woodblock cutter naps,
Trees grow as in early summer,
No means "promise," *chih* means "advent."

Translator's notes:
1. The brand of Japanese sake meaning "crane from the marshland."

2. Japanese pronunciation of "crane from the marshland."

Somewhat

The rain falls far in a realm unknown
In a realm opposite to my desire.
This is called the *aware* of rain.

Somewhat like a pilgrim's incense
Flickering in running water—
That was the evening
You passed many villages
With different apparel,
Different festivities
And different languages
(You were just passing through)—
A light frost in your heart,
Your expression failed to hide the ebb and flow
Of surprise and joy on your face.

Somewhat like the wind
Rushing in a hood and stayed—
You unknotted the scarf
Tied at Rainbow City that morning,
Let the coconut trees' fans caress you,
"This must be your hometown,"
And I answered yes.
When the evening sun burned
Outside the red pavilion of the medical school,
Inside, there remained a silence,
A serious, silent civilization
Your face sanctioned.

Somewhat like an uneasy rest, mid-journey,
Dragonflies flew above the Chungshan North Road,
You praised the blue mountain in another tongue,
With ancient, other eyes, you watched the rain.
Somewhat, seemed to ponder
Beyond the orderly metaphor:

"Michi no ryoiki ni ame wa huru
Watashi no yokubo no hantaigawa no ryoiki ni
Kore o ame no aware to yu."[1]

1. Translator's note: this is the Japanese version of the beginning three lines of the poem.

Loneliness

Loneliness is an elderly beast
Hiding among the rocks in my mind,
His back, a chameleon design,
I know, protectively colors his race.
Dreary are his eyes, forever after
The floating clouds far away,
Longing, too, to stretch and wander
In the sky;
Contemplating, he lowers his head,
Lets the storm freely lash
The missing violence of his shed skins,
The petrified passion given him with time.

Loneliness is an elderly beast
Hiding among the rocks in my mind;
At thunder strike, he moves slowly,
Clumsily walks into my wine glass;
His infatuated eyes
Sadly gaze at an evening drinker,
This time, I know, he regrets
His rash departure from familiar storms
For the chill of this wine.
My glass at my lips,
I kindly accept him.

Chi Tzu of Yen Ling Hangs Up His Sword[1]

Constantly I hear the mountain's deep grievances.
At first I drifted at will,
How can I sort an indifferent
History of coming and going?
All right, all right,
Let me close my eyes and dance for you;
Desolate water reeds, chilly cresent moon,
A late foreign evening, the cloth-poundings of a washerwoman
Bite at my shadow's heels,
Chafe my outworn swordsmanship.
What? A long forgotten scar on my forearm;
It will only redden,
Like a sunset flower by the river,
During my rapture with wine.

Then, we sat idly in the scorching sun—
A pair of dwindling lotus stems,
Before my northern expedition.
Saddest, now, was that approaching summer,
Oh! Those delicate singings of the southern girls!
Who uses their sewing thread
And the nibbling pains of needles
To make me draw my sword from its scabbard
And promise my southern return, to give my sword
To you . . .
How could I sort—
The northern beauties, the Ch'i-Lu scholars,
The *Book of Songs*
Left me a Confucian,
And forgetful.

After stopping sword practice, how could I realize
(The legend continued, you thought of me and died)
What only the seven holes of the flute
Still gloomily tell of my disillusionment with the mainland?

In my early years,
Archery, horsemanship, saber and sword
Exceeded speech, silenced rhetoric.
But, since Confucius wandered in foreign lands,
Since Tzu Lu died abruptly, and Tzu Sha entered Wei,
We rushed helter-skelter to the great lords' mansions.
This is why I gave up my sword,
Bound my hair,
Studied the *Book of Songs,*
And appeared as an eloquent scholar . . .

Oh! Scholar!
The scholar breaks his wrist
At your darkening cemetery woods.
Never again am I knight-errant, or Confucian;
Only the tarnish of this sword
Will speak highly of us in quiet autumnal night;
You died of longing for a friend,
I sicken as a fisherman, a woodcutter;
The tired boatman,
I, who was once arrogant, and humble.

1. Translator's note: in volume 31 of *The Records of the Grand Historian (Shih Chih),* the Grand Historian narrates the following friendship tale: "Chi Cha was making his northern expedition to serve his first embassy. He met his friend, Hsu, on the way. Hsu liked Chi's sword very much, but he was too shy to say so. Chi knew Hsu liked the sword, but because of his mission to a powerful state, he did not give the sword to Hsu. When he returned, Hsu had already died. Chi took off his sword, hung it on the tree by Hsu's grave, and left. His follower asked, 'Hsu is already dead, who do you want to give the sword to?' Chi answered, 'Nevertheless, since I have set my mind to give my sword to him, how can his death change my mind.'"

MS. Found in a Bottle

Beyond these cypresses,
I see the sun setting in the west. At this hour,

The tides arrive at this shore. Yet I know only that
Every tide starts from Hualien. In those days,
I was once astonished and asked,
"Would there be a seashore far away?"
At this moment, the other seashore
Is this one,
And only the dwindling starlight remains.

Only the starlight
Shines on my spent sentiments now,
And my voice touches the rushing tides,
"Do you think of the shores of Hualien?"

I wonder with every roaring tide
Rushing to the shores of Hualien,
After they turn back,
How many summers will they take to arrive here.
I believe it must have been a sudden determination
To become involved, and once they turn,
Their fate is determined. Here comes
The same wave, flowing quietly to this deserted shore.

If I sit silently and listen to the tides,
Observing every shape of each tide,
And trying to portray my future,
Look at the small one to my left,
Are those ephemeral fish eggs?
Or, this fair-shaped wave,
Perhaps it is sea-weed;
And the large one far away,
Maybe those are flying fish,
Leaping in the summer night.

When a wave rushes in to this desolate shore,
I wonder what would be best to do?
Maybe it's still best to turn myself into a wave,
With a sudden leap and turn, and a return current,
I would join the quiet sea,
Would overflow onto the shores of Hualien.

And yet when I start walking into the sea,
The weight of the water sustains,
But its volume will increase,
And the beach over there
Will subside just inland.
As I walk further and even drown myself
Seven feet west of this desolate shore,
Will Hualien in the month of June,
Oh! Will Hualien again spread the rumor
Of another tidal wave?

Translator's note: the poem's title is also the title of Yang's collection of poems, which reminds us of Poe's work.

From "The Sonnets"

11.

I want you to come rushing in the wind,
Passing through the path lined with withered azaleas,
I want you to peep into my frustrated garden,
Like tiptoed tiny starlets, with shoes in your hands,
Or to set a fire to diminish autumn
With your flushing afternoon cheek, like a ripened fruit
Burning away my frustrated autumn garden;
I want you to come rushing in the wind,
Passing through my bubbling veins,
Now you are a gunboat porting where you will,
Cutting, churning the many placid shores.
You are a star rushing in the wind,
Passing through my clotted fortress;

In the rain of arrows, you sing and run,
I want you to come to me rushing in the gusty wind.

From "The Sonnets"

12.

I want you to come rushing in the rain,
Passing through the muddied city corner
And the wavering trees;
I want you to become the new tumbling autumn winds
And enamor the fruit about to all;
Maybe you are the fruit,
Hesitating and in distress in the afternoon,
Wondering at which angle you will fall this time.
Oh! So many considerations!
Finally, you fall vertically
And always on the greenish lawn.
I want you to come rushing in the rain,
Passing through last spring's garden,
Where a peppermint was buried
And a bonsai withered—
I cannot let you come alone in this heavy rain.

A Night Song: How To Defend Against Tree Shadows

A team of crushed tree shadows
Will invade your window abruptly

Ahead of your consciousness.
But they say it does not matter,
As long as the shadows don't leave footprints on the snow,
And retreat punctually, without noise.

If they leave footprints on the snow
Like tracks of the white bears
Then plant sparsely some honeysuckles, cool and low;
If only honeysuckles invade,
It will be still all right,
Because it is possible to lift the curtains,
And make fire in the house.

This is how you can get rid of them.
But if they rush into your house
And storm at your bed with years past
Why not entertain them with your new wine
And seal scripts?
They say the invading tree shadows
Are most afraid of wine and pre-Ch'in artifacts.

Yu Kuang-chung (1928–   )

Like evergreen foliage, the lengthy span of Yu Kuang-chung's creative life glows with lively luster. The multiple facets of his poetic style aternate from Western models to Chinese antiquity. Despite his fecund creativity, Yu maintains a consistently perfect poetic diction and style; though a risk-taker, he calculates his risks, and his innovations do not result from rash experimentation.

The free flow of his creative life reflects events through his lifetime. After teaching at National Normal University for a couple of years, he lectured and toured in the United States between 1961 and 1966, under the sponsorship of the State Department. Three years later, he left for Colorado and taught at Temple Bell College for two years. In 1974, he moved to Hong Kong to teach at the Chinese University. In recent years, he has shuttled between Taiwan and Hong Kong, intrigued with the awkward situation the Chinese in Hong Kong are encountering, and increasingly saddened for the two Chinas, mainland and Taiwan. After an absence of 11 years, Yu returned in 1985 to teach in Taiwan.

Poetry:

Sad Songs of the Boatman, 1952
Blue Feathers, 1954
Stalactite, 1960
Halloween, 1960
Association of the Lotus, 1965
A Youth from Wu-ling, 1967
Night Market of the Heavenly Kingdom, 1969
Music Percussive, 1969

White Jade Bitter Melon

—collected by the Palace Museum of Taiwan

Half in slumber, half awake, gently aglow
As though slowly waking from a thousand-year sleep,
A melon ripens and mellows,
A bitter melon, once.
Time has ground out a deep, impregnating transparency;
See the twirling beard of roots
And the caressing palms of leaves.
The harvest of that year
Was a hungry sucking of the inexhaustible milk, old China.
Such a perfect rotund smoothness,
Such overfull satisfaction;
A touch to reach incessantly out, to expand,
To harden all cheese-white grapes,
Is the tip of the melon, erecting its old freshness.

A China has contracted into a map,
In youth, you do not know how to fold it up,
And let its vastness endlessly stretch
Like your remembrance of mother, and her breast;
You stoop to her fecundity,
Roots of you grope for her nourishment.

Greatly patient and kind
She nourished this lucky or unlucky offspring
Transporting to a bitter melon all his mainland love.
On a land boots have trampled, horses have trampled,
Heavy tank belts have trampled,
Without scars.

But through this glass case, a miracle still
Carries the blessing from the mainland,
Ripening in wonderful light,[1] beyond time,
In a self-sufficient universe,
Full and without decay,
A fairy fruit from this world,
But not from fairyland.
Your old form
And the crafty hands put to it had decayed;
With a thousand glimpses of examination
The craftsman transformed you and laughed
At your wandering spirit in the white jade.
Like a song, praising life as a melon and bitter,
Transformed eternally to bear sweetness.

---

1. Translator's note: the author is using a pun on his given name, Kuang-chung, which means "in midst of light."

The Cricket and the Machine Gun

Say, who's going to win
The debate between
A cricket and a machine gun?
The machine gun, of course—
With its speedy, vigorous eloquence,

Its fiery tongue, dazzling teeth—
A notorious debate champion.
At its roar, mountains echo
Ta-ta-ta, hollowly, like applause.
Crickets are speechless, I presume,
Unless the gunsmoke disperses, the gunbarrels cool
And the gunsight idly points to the void;
Unless the echoes suddenly cease
And gunshells fall like pine nuts over the ground.
Then, in the quiet following magnificence,
A soft voice floats over the heroes' gravesites,
Among the cat tails it leisurely chants
An address to the attentive night.
Perhaps the singer endures;
A machine gun proves itself with shrill whisltes,
A cricket uses only its silence.

Nostalgia

When I was small,
Nostalgia was a tiny postage stamp,
I, on this side,
My mother, on the other.

When I grew up,
Nostalgia was a narrow ship ticket,
I, on the other end of
My bride.

Later on,
Nostalgia was a low tomb,
I, outside.
My mother, inside.

And now,
Nostalgia is the coastline of a shallow strait.
I, on this side,
Of the mainland.

An Old Woman in Mongkok

She is even more old-fashioned than Mongkok, the market,
Even older, is her native accent,
And much more, her native land.
Her vegetable roots entwining her native land,
Her tongue twisting her native language,
The old woman's relatives are soil and dialect.
Her trembling hands are red as the sweet potatoes
She weighs for me in a catty—
Children nursed and raised by the kind old soil.

Elusive dialect, accents of T'ang-Sung,
Tangy soils, once the farmlands of Chou-Han;
That from her lips, that on her hands, I seem to know
By her numbling local gait of tongue, but am at a loss.
I know only the rippling eyes
Deep in the wrinkles when she smiles,
Eyes once my aunt's and grandmother's;
The face and twittering accent
Of every old woman by the well, before the stove,
In every river village and mountain district in the South.

I approach and enter, those eyes
Becoming my roots and my fairy tales.

Sea Offerings

Author's note: According to the *South China Morning Post* in Hong Kong, many of the refugees who fled from Canton and swam to Hong Kong were attacked mercilessly by sharks in the Big Roc Bay. By September 1974, one hundred and eleven of them had died. Survivors lost arms and legs. The South Sea was originally infested with sea fiends and monsters. Crocodiles plagued the rivers and lakes of Swatow. That prompted Han Yu, the Governor, to compose his "Offering to the Crocodiles," and to order the exodus of the crocodiles within seven days. A thousand years later, the crocodiles left, but the sharks came. To Han Yu, crocodiles were merely guilty of being "fiercely restless in unruly ponds, having stayed and devoured commoners' cattle to fatten themselves, multiplying their broods and challenging the authority of the local Governor." Thus the sharks, which obstruct the road to freedom, are more guilty. My "Sea Offerings" is, on the one hand, to mourn the dead, and on the other, to reproach the ruthless creatures. Let it be, then, my "Offerings to the Sharks."

Oh! Great South China Sea with boundless magnificent outward
     ocean,
Wind will not blow away
The swirling currents
A thousand fathoms deep
Beneath a face veil of beautiful blue gauze;
How many lake fiends and sea monsters were tossed aside
In tumbling onward-rushing tides pushing the old universe?
Stars brighten, stars dim,
The moon rises, falls,
Multicolored ship flags in gusty winds.
How many navies can this big cradle rock?
The same blue and briny depth
Cast big junks southward six hundred years ago,
Broad-beamed boats, one after the other,
Imperial pennants shone on each other,
Masts pointed to windy clouds over the Indian Ocean
Unreachable, far beyond the horizon.

In bygone ages, you once floated
Su Shih, but drowned Wang Po,
Provoked the literary giant in T'ang,
Local governor of Swatow,
To angrily wield his brush
And expell the ruthless creatures to the South Sea.
Muddy waves crashing, they cleanse themselves
Every thousand years,
Resolute are the clear sandy beaches and rocky shores
Today.

"The sharks are coming; Sharks!"
This new curse is
Upon you nakedly, upon your helplessness,
Upon sore arms and legs, cramped muscles,
Lacerations by wild sea plants;
The brine pinches, foams, slashes your eyes,
As you brave the tides and wind.
You drift to Hong Kong,
To a mirage of fairy islands and mysterious cities,
Swim further, toward a fascinating horizon, and—
"The sharks are coming!"
A black curse! Warm currents turn swimmers chilled and trem-
    bling
"The sharks come!"
A fin splits the water into
Epileptic foams, a splashing half acre of blue shrieks,
Shivering cold are the two canine rows of wolf
Rushing the coming tide, horrible jaws open,
Blade to blade, in glittering violence.
A choked cry surprised at the flashing pain,
Another warm body bids a naked farewell
To the misty horizon, to freedom, oh!
After twitches, after spasms and
Loosened shoulders, shiny leg muscles loosened up,
A sea burial, half way
Spreads a bloody banner,

Entombs on the watery surface
Disappearing in an eddy
Only the remaining black hair, tangled with seaweed.

Young swimmer
in thin skin,
Your vigor circulates
From toes to fingers,
To compete against the tumbling blue outside;
Scorching sun burns your skin to copper
In the surveillance of Autumn's heat.
Beneath a tree, other youths
Sip orangeade, or iced tea in cool green shade,
Or loose their long soft snores from bamboo mats
To echo the incessant cicadas outside the window screen;
You took, instead,
The choking brine;
Chose between the bitter sea or bitter land.
At the choice, you were pickled in one night
Into a cucumber; with hair and eyebrows,
You stumbled onto the craggy shore,
Your blood dripping on oyster shells;
You slipped on the green moss and got up.
The Big Roc Bay contained and
Handed you to the sea and sky.
You deeply breathed,
Then deeply swallowed a sea journey,
Putting all search lights, all patrol boats
Police dogs, and sharks,
Putting all possible bewilderment at landing, or the
Despair of return
And all your naked nineteen years
Into a single bet!
These years are what your mother gave you.
You once retraced that mist of road
With all tracks leading south; your frightened steps said
The mainland is where the eagle soars low,

The ocean is where seagulls cry,
The native land has rancid soil, smelly grass.
Farewell, childhood, farewell to
What is but a nap beneath a banyan tree.
Farewell, sad days of Cultural Revolution!

Oh, young man, the breaking waves splash like your breaking
    tears,
The limbs of a long-distance swimmer stroke and strive like fins,
The chest sticks out in the wide sea,
The lungs bellow, the waves bellow,
Against a cold blue sea spreads the seething crimson
Primitive human, against divine primitivism;
Shields, trophies, flashlights blinking,
These are not the best prizes,
That is freedom.
That waits for him at the other end of the bitter sea.
Is it really freedom there,
Or an exile's fairy island?
Are heavy shadows of skyscrapers going to fall young dreams?
A fish cleaver hews a bloody path,
Police sirens everywhere.
This last flip of the coin is life, or death,
Is not the vows of young boys and girls under moonlight praying
    at a murmuring fountain;
This is the South Sea, wide open for
The entrance and exit of all sea monsters,
Tiger sharks, white sharks freely come and go,
Fins combing the unpredictable tides,
Jaws rowed with blind saws.
Deep is the South Sea
From here to Luson, Brunei, and Sumatra;
The sea god generously receives all aquatics,
Tiny shrimp, crabs, huge whales.
Tatooed murderers!
Even should you not learn kindness from dolphins
Who rescue from the sinking ships their travelers,

At least heed the guilt of crocodiles
Who wagged their hideous tails under string bows and poisoned
    arrows,
Who made their exile to the waters of South Asia.
Do you think I lack bow and arrow?
My brush cannot touch the gods?
There is no road to freedom?
It is this, a spacious blue field,
Where nothing obstructs
You unclaimed wild dogs,
You dirtiest criminals;
My dirge will record your crimes
So all sea creatures will shame your company;
Not a turtle or dragon will swim with you;
Governor Han was long dead, but Swatow is near,
In his temple still his spirit dominates;
Away! While the tides ebb tonight
Follow your cousin crocodile and lead all your brood
Southward! The high sea is boundless
In the serpent's cave, or the dragon's palace;
Numerous treasures will fill your empty stomachs
And quench the blood thirst of your jaws;
You can feed on ink squirts beneath the sea
Or pirates and opium men above.

Vengeful ghosts squeak
In the bitter sea's heart;
The late tides are aroused.
After the lights are extinguished in the sea market,
People sleep; ghosts are awake,
Dim flickers among fishing boats,
Green like the will-o'-the-wisp;
Listen! Upon the water dark and deep
Float mutilated ghosts,
Hairs entangled
Fingernails gripping broken air cushions, balloons and lifebuoys,
Squeak, squeak, they struggle and gasp,

Squeak, squeak, "The sharks come!"
They fail the paradise ahead,
They fail the land behind;
In poor Big Roc Bay
They have no advance or return;
Even the vengeful corpses shred into wandering ghosts
With no burial,
Float and drift on the waves
Between shores.

Oh, sea god,
Be you spiritual, powerful,
Summon your blood-thirsty sharpshooters
And infamous submarines,
Summon them back to their troops,
And pity these crippled drifting ghosts in their blue public ceme-
    tery,
Oh, sea god,
That they rest!

The Kowloon-Canton Railway

How do I feel about Hong Kong?
Your tiny aerogramme in my hand, I bitterly grin.
Hong Kong, my friend, is a jangling beat
Playing on the railroad with a thousand wheels;
Toward, from, the border
Sunrise to sunset,
Northbound, southbound,
Playing over and over an endless border tuned to nostalgia.
Scissors cannot sever
Nor wheels grind
A helpless umbilical cord

Stretching to the vast north;
This maternal body
So close, but so new!
This land
So attached, but so unrelated!
An old cradle softly rocking, far away,
Your memory, my friend, and mine,
Memories like neurons stretched
Sensitive, to this railroad.
Now I stand briefly at a depot,
Your letter in my hand, and lean on the pole.
Listen!
Eyes closed
I still hear the crisp knocking passenger train,
The heavily humming rumbling freight cars.
That rank, stifling smell upon is—
Quick! hold your breath—
The pig train.

After My Fiftieth Birthday

Five feet three inches,
The top of my head is in the snow line.
Sparse spots in this black pine forest are white.
Early whiteness, though fearful,
Is not surrender, but binds mortals to immortals.
Black I came from mother,
But white from metamorphosis, the strict stepmother.
Since the old days, too many heroes faced mirrors
Frightened of the chilly, snowy peaks.
They dared not ascend alone
Not knowing peaks of lonely whiteness at dusk
Led to death; or eternity.

Complain of my old age? I won't.
I am proud to come above sea level;
The long road lets me check the horse:
If I am old, I will not abide my stable.
Inquire my horsepower,
But lend me your ear, please,
And listen to the flames in my breast,
To the bursting volcano beneath the peak,
To the seething, churning engine
Almost out of control in
Gallop. Four hundred horsepower.

To a Painter

They told me
This summer,
You plan to travel far away,
To see Van Gogh, or Hsu Pei-hung,
With your easel and grey hair,
Big laughter, and Szechuan accent.

Should you leave, my friend, Taipei would be empty,
Long streets, narrow lanes; no one to see you turning back
In this rainy season, unfit for traveling.
Black umbrellas spot the sky,
Yellow mud is the road,
Why not wait 'til mid-autumn?

Only the rice paddies of Southern Taiwan did you release,
Those village temples, water buffaloes—
And once it's evening in summer
One or two egrets in summer
Always reminded of something, fly up

From your splash-ink paintings.

Pine Waves

Long summer, perpetual days;
Deep mountain like an old bell,
How much quietude fills
Such enormity: round and void?
When the recluse of the mountain
Comes, his long sleeves elegantly waver,
Caressing rows and rows of the lofty, ancient pines along the cor-
    ridor;
What he plays softly, casually
On an emerald zither with a thousand strings,
Unceasingly shakes bundles and bundles of tenuous pine needles;
As in the low rumblings of a tidal wave,
So shake the pines like tides on a far away coast:
Such heavenly music!
How abruptly impromptu for the empty mountain!
Which with unleashed emotion, freely rises and falls.
Who or what can detain the fleeting robes and beard of the im-
    mortal?

Listen. Now.
The joyful recluse
Plucks and plays his way
To the other side of the mountain.

Lo Fu (1928–   )

An early major strength in promoting Chinese poetry in Taiwan was a group of military personnel who gathered around the *Epoch Poetry Quarterly*. These poets include Lo Fu, Ya Hsien, Chang Mo, Kuan Kuan, Shang Ch'in, Yang Ling-yeh, Hsin Yu, and other soldier-poets. Lo Fu, a leader in the group, has a firm grasp of language and presents the most powerful imagery. Moreover, he often mutilates his language, creating violent images. These practices are best demonstrated in his collection, *Death of the Stony Cell*. In 1974, after the publication of *Enchanted Songs*, Lo Fu released himself from the bondage of nihilistic existentialism, moving toward a clear expression of themes. The growth of his nostalgia and his learning of the death of his mother in the mainland, from whom he was long separated, have prompted him to write of more defined, realistic themes.

Poetry:

Spiritual River, 1957
Death of the Stony Cell, 1965
Beyond, 1967
River without Embankment, 1970
Enchanted Songs, 1974
Clamoring of the Lotus, 1975
The Wounds of Time, 1981
The Brewing Stone, 1983

The Crab-legged Flower

Perhaps you shouldn't be sad because of what happened

Crab-legged flowers bursting about the rim of an earthen bowl
In quietude, all turn their heads at once.
By the window, your hand gestures
In a dark crimson desperation,
In the entanglement of blue veins,
And you start to say:
Naked!
Then, with an overflowing of body fragrance,
A petal bulges,
Then another.

Crab-legged flowers
Lie across the sky of your forehead,
Covering it all.

In the sweetest moment,
You start to say:
Pain!
Leaves and branches uncurl,
The sound of water running from a stem
Stupifies you;
In the flowers' blooming like opening wounds
You recognize yourself.

Water

To flow is a verb,
Not to flow is a noun;
The sum of water and sky
Is a well,
Plus our faces

Equals the gush from a wound:
Watch out!

Peeling Pears at Midnight

Chilly and thirsty,
Silent, I stare
At a Korean pear
On a midnight tea-stand.

That is really
An icy
Bronze-colored
Pear.

Slit in half, it has
Deep in its chest,
Such a deep, deep well.

Trembling, with my thumb and index finger,
I pick up a sliver of pear.

White innocence.

My knife drops.
I bend down to find
Oh! All over the floor
Peelings of my bronze-colored skin.

Having Followed the Sound of Rain
into the Mountain But Found No Rain

Carrying a parasol and singing
"The plums are sour in March,"

I am the one pair of grass sandals
In the mountains.

A woodpecker pecks
Empty, hollow echoes;
A tree in pain twirls upward;
I enter the mountain
But find no rain;
My parasol flutters around a blue rock.
There, a man holds his head, sits
Watching the end of his cigarette turn to ash.

I descend the mountain,
But find no rain.
Three pine cones roll down from the road-sign to my feet;
I pick them up,
But they turn out to be a handful of bird cries.

Beyond Logic

Do you know why rivers grip their banks tightly?
They have only one way to die.
Even a boat is choiceless between two banks.
We would rather take an incendiary bomb
Than the smell of a burnt, setting sun.

To live is to be destined to accept the goddamned sonnet,
Even to the turning of the last page
There is that fucking sonnet.

This is the public cemetery;
Only a person's voice is buried here,
Echoes in the mind.
Eagles soar over the cliff.
If it were a thorn, let it be loved by blood;
If poppies, let it be a smile on the lips.
The poet's existential creed is not to die.

After Dawn

Pushing away last night violently
I repel my tickles,
I hold up my arms and let
My temperature rush to the roof through my fingers
To become the cry of a man.

First to wake is the overnight bed,
The second, my daughter's dark eyebrows
        jumping left across her forehead
         to the right;
Only the red lotus on her slippers
Still sets its sail. . .

Blood wakes from blood
As light wakes from phosphorous;
Oh, hanging on the wall
The old man fishing in river snow,
Throws over the lure
That my wife catches with half-opened eyes.

I open the curtains,
The morning pours in like wine,
The sun rushes to the wall clock
Biting right on the six-thirty of our house.

The Brewing Stone

A wintry night,
Stealthily we buried the stone,
And you said,
"When spring comes,
It will brew new wine."

That year
nearly all the rice fields lay sterile.

Snow-piled childhood
Melts so quickly.
Fortunately, I still am hot stone
When you hold me in your hand.

Translator's note: the poet confided in the Afterword of his poetry album that "The Brewing Stone" came from his childhood belief that burying a pumpkin would brew wine. Lo Fu and his younger brothers did this. After three days, they found that the buried pumpkin had already turned to stone. They knew it must have been the trick of neighborhood kids who wanted to revenge the theft of their pumpkin.

Early Snow

In the city
We anticipated its coming abruptly, the shivering,
I mean, that kind of white
Below zero.
The snow
Actually fell early in midnight
On daisies blooming like little young wives.
Last night, it fell.
That kind of white, aye,
That kind of purity
Is the scenery we have long awaited.
Yet, because it is pure,
I don't want it to come soon
Nor melt soon,
Like the orchid you've planted
Should not bloom early
Nor wither early.

To Mr. Hsiao Ch'ien

From cow-stall to Iowa,
From Rightist to lovable capitalism
The route is a little too long.
Even you walk to your *Setting Sun,*
But find no *Valley of Dreams.*
On the left bank of the Mississippi,
In a cooling sunset
Your long shadow
Falls more autumnal than the maple leaves.
It was said you brought a bottle of Mao-t'ai,
Very high proof;
And that the China weekend in Iowa is pretty high proof.
I trust the laughters of the seminar hostess
Also were.
You made your first toast
With few words;
You spoke to the world with wounds.
Let's not talk literature,
But weather.
In Peking, it may begin to snow;
Here in Iowa, it's already deep autumn;
In Taiwan, the sun shines really bright,
The warmth is just right for you.

Author's note: on September 15, 1979, the University of Iowa sponsored a three-day China Weekend, and a seminar titled "The Future of Chinese Literary Writings." Some twenty persons from mainland China, overseas, and Taiwan participated. The mainland writers were headed by Hsiao Ch'ien, who early in his career wrote the two novels, *Setting Sun*, and *Valley of Dreams*.

Watching the Native Country from the Border

—For Yu Kuang-chung

We talked and talked,
And unconsciously came to the Horse Dismounting Bay.

The mist just beginning to rise,
We suddenly stopped, aware,
And our hands started to sweat.
The binoculars brought us a sharp, nearby nostalgia.
My hair scattered in the wind
And my vision tightened as a heart might beat, as
A distant mountain flew in my face,
Knocked me down
And heavily bruised me.

I was sick, sick
Like the withering cluster of azaleas on the slope.
One flower remained, spewing blood and
Bending behind a notice board:
"No Crossing the Frontier."
Then
A white egret suddenly flapped its wings, shocked
From the rice paddies; it flew across the border town
And abruptly back.

Then, the cuckoo's fiery
Smokey calls,
Sound after sound,
Pierced the chilly spring in a foreign land.
I smoldered, my eyes all red, blood seething,
But you lifted the collar of your coat,
Turned and asked,
"Are you chilly or not?"

After Thundered Insects, it's Vernal Equinox;
The Ch'ing-ming Festival should be nearby.
I surprisingly understood the Cantonese accent.
When rain had rendered the brown earth
Into greenish language,
Look, you said,
Beyond Fook-tin Village was Shui-wei,
The soil of my native country, in reachable distance.
I caught only a handful of cold mist.

Author's note: in March of 1979 I went to Hong Kong upon invitation. On the morning
of the 16th, my friend, Yu Kuang-chung, drove me to take a look at the borderline of
Horse Dismounting Bay. It was misty, but I could make out my native country with the
binoculars. There were also the heartbreaking cuckoo calls I had not heard for many
years. In my mind at this moment must have been what is called the timid feeling of
nostalgia.

Song of the Cricket

Someone once said, "Overseas, I heard a cricket sing, and
thought it was the one I heard when I was in the coun-
tryside of Szechuan."

Carrying from the courtyard
To the corner of the wall:
Jit, jut . . . Jit, jut.
Out of the stone crevice
Suddenly jumping
To a pillow under the white hairs,
Jut, jut.
Pushed from yesterday's drifting
To this day's corner of the world,
The cricket sings
But hides its head, its legs, wings.

I grope everywhere,
High in the sky, deep in the earth.
Still it is invisible.
I even tear open my breast,
But fail to find that vibrator.
The evening rain just then stopped.
The moon outside the window
Delivers the axe sound of a woodcutter.
The stars are seething,
And the cricket's song bubbling
Like a stream.
My childhood drifts from upstream,
But tonight I am not in Ch'en-tu,
And my snores do not mean nostalgia.
Unceasing is the cricket song in my ears,
A thousand-threaded tune;
I have forgotten the year, the month, the evening,
Which city or town,
In which bus depot I have heard this song.
Jut, jut . . . Jit, jut.
Tonight, however, more shocking.
The cricket's cry
Meanders like River Chai-ling by my pillow,
Deep in night,
With no boat to hire;
I can only swim, follow the tides
Where the waves of the Three Gorges are sky-high
And monkeys shriek by the river bank,
And fish,
Only hot spicy bean fish lie in a green porcelain platter.
Jut, jut.
Which cricket is really singing?
The Cantonese one sings the loneliest,
The Szechuan the saddest,
And the Peking cricket, the noisiest.
But the Hunan cricket sings
With the taste of spicy heat.

Yet, what finally woke me
Was that one in the lane at San-chang Li,
The softest, the dearest
Singing of all.

Cheng Ch'ou-yu (1933–   )

Cheng Ch'ou-yu's poetry has reflected the thirty years' develop-
ment of modern poetry in Taiwan, but to a limited extent, since
the poet stopped writing in 1965 and did not resume until after
more than ten years. Though powerful, his recent poems are not
as captivating as his earlier poems, most of which are widely read
and frequently quoted. Cheng's legendary appearance, disappear-
ance, and reappearance can be taken as representative of the hope-
despair-new hope cycle of modern poetry in Taiwan.

His poetic language represents a conscious effort to link
his poems with the modern lyrical tradition in China, particularly
the lyrics of Hsin Ti. Cheng's poems combine the mainland with
Taiwan, and classical restraint with romantic release. All his "fa-
mous" lines are shocking not only in their means of expression,
but also in their degree of emotion. He currently teaches Chinese
at Yale University.

Poetry:

Upon the Dreamland, 1955
To Pass on the Mantle, 1966
Slave Girl Outside the Window, 1968
Long Songs, 1968
Selected Poems, 1974
Selected Poems I, 1979
Journey of a Yen Native, 1980
The Possibility of Snow, 1985
Selected Poems of Cheng Ch'ou-yu, 1986

The Rain Says

—For the children in Chinese soil: A song

(The rain says,
April has already waited for a long while on earth.)

Fields and pastures have waited long enough,
As have fish ponds and brooks;
When fields have chilled a winter's encaged seeds,
And seared pastures have lost the tracks of cattle,
When shallow fish ponds have stagnated fish
And small brooks are voiceless, songless,
The rain says,
I am coming,
I come to visit the great earth of April.

I am coming, I stroll lightly
And gently speak,
My silken love has woven a universe,
I coo to every child his pet name, sweetly, precisely;
I am coming
Clamorless, without lightning
Or rushing wind.
Perhaps, you'll know my approach
But don't spread your parasol of rejection,
Don't close the window, nor lower your curtain,
Don't rush to your straw raincoat
Your straw hat.

The rain says,
I come to the great earth to be near,
A friend of April bearing the baptism of spring;
Why not lift your face and let me kiss you,
Why not follow me, walking the same beats of my steps.

Follow and walk on the balmy fields,
Into pastures budding with honeysuckles,

Around the pond to greet leaping fishes;
Listen to the brooks' new ballads of washerwomen.

The rain says,
I am coming, from far away I come.
There, steep mountains rise,
White clouds crowd the sky;
As you, I was once a child full of play,
But I am lucky
Who grew up happily in the blankets of a cloud.

Your first lesson: Learn how to laugh boldly;
Don't you know
When willows see me
They madly laugh themselves to their knees;
When stone lions see me,
They madly laugh into tears;
When little swallows see me,
They laugh and slant their wings.
Your second lesson: The same.
When the flag sees me,
It clamors in boisterous laughters,
And once it does, then
There is the voice of spring.
Once you laugh boldly, the
Hope of the earth is there.

The rain says, I am coming,
And having arrived, I will stay.
When you laugh freely, I happily rest;
One day, when you eat your apple and wipe your mouth,
Know your lesson. That sweet taste
Is my heart's blessing.

Ladder-climbing and Grocery

Talking of houses, cars and kids;
Rains echo, sighs dripping through the eave-gutter.

Talking of careers, marketability,
Of an overseas conference,
A new suburban restaurant. Quite a place for gourmets
(He sips his tea and extinguishes his cigarette.)

Talking of Maryland crab, trout of the Green Bay,
Of black bass, yellowtails,
But the mention of the Fishing Island Incident
Shut everyone's mouth.

The rain sighed more heavily. . .
Water splashed up from cars passing,
Who was it turned on the porch light so suddenly?
And were the bundles of silvery lights plunging
Arrows bouncing back from the blue void?

(He had to leave
In the heavy rain)
Talking of buying groceries on his way. . .

I had to ponder.
A mature scientist,
Isn't he something like a ripening honeydew melon
Far from its soil, tagged with a supermarket price,
Isn't he exactly the grocery in the Westerner's list?

Author's note: ladder-climbing (*p'a-t'i*) is a pun for "party" in Chinese, an upclimbing exercise in which you very often come across the elite: scientists, physicians, engineers, etc.

Abode of the Roaming Immortals

(Yosemite)

Give to a little fairy a little mountain,
And an eleven-foot cascade.
A pine stands by the cliff,
And, there, another, taller.
Just higher is the ashram
Where the Taoist lives in celibacy,
Who never planned to marry, anyway.
On the other side of the stream
Is the little mountain;
The little fairy
Happy chemist
Mingles daily his laughters with his magic herbs.

Gateway Arch

The sun falls perpendicularly west
In this vastness; there is no return road;
Further south is long-grassed Oklahoma.
Where the whole tribe moved in exodus
(Who tipped off the trail to the enemy?)
That following year.
A year earlier
The tribesmen had executed the great chief McIntosh.

The capital had sent another general,
Wagons had rolled and rolled over Illinois plains,
Cornfields all were ripened
When the thunderstorms stopped.

All baptized Christians bent down in the Missouri
Shivering with watery reflections,
Their bodies a gleaming row, like God's shiny sickles.

It was concluded,
This plot between men and their God;
The harvest—the whole procedure of thanksgiving
And the sun to the west,
Making golden the torso solemnly standing,
A sickle to swish like winds;
The crimson splash of the sunset shocked Mother earth.
The sun sank in a complete and dead silence, on
The chieftan's bow
Held high in the European's hands,
A tribute and
Forever the arch of triumphant invasion.

Author's note: Gateway Arch is a steel arch standing in St. Louis, Missouri, where the Mississippi and Missouri meet. It symbolizes the colonial pioneering westward. In 1830, five highly civilized Indian tribes were forced to move along the Atlantic coast, then west to Oklahoma. Thousands of the Indians died on the road by ransacking and massacres. The trip was called "the trail of tears." William McIntosh, chieftain of the Lower Creek tribe which signed the treaty to lease lands to the American Confederacy, was later executed by his tribesmen in 1825.

Ya Hsien (1932–   )

It has been more than fifteen years since Ya Hsien published his last collection of poetry, *Abyss.* Yet for all these years his poems have helped blaze the trail for the development of modern Chinese poetry in Taiwan. Ya Hsien is among the very few modern poets who have blended successfully the lyrical tradition of the 1930s in the mainland, particularly the lyrics of Ho Ch'i-fang, with the writing of modern lyrics in Taiwan. Ya's poems possess a sweet cadence, an ironic tone, and a narrative mode. He is capable of using northern colloquialisms to present characters and events of the tragic past. While the long narrative poem "Abyss" was often hailed as his existential rendering of the modern Chinese mind, his other short lyrics are an attempt to break away from the dullness of the vernacular language, opening up the imaginative faculties of the poetic mind. He has written about exotic cities—Babylon, Jerusalem, Rome, Paris, Chicago, Naples—but had visited none prior to leaving for Iowa in 1966. Since 1977, he has been the chief editor of the literary supplement to the *United Daily News* and an indispensable promoter of modern Chinese literature in Taiwan. He completed his graduate studies at the University of Wisconsin.

Poetry:

Collected Poems, 1959
Abyss, 1968; rev. ed. 1971
Salt (English translations), 1968
Collected Poems of Ya Hsien, 1981

An Opera Songstress

Since sixteen, her name has drifted in the city.
Quite a sad tune.

Rather eunuchs had guarded those almond arms,
And that petite coiffure broken the hearts of the Mandarins.

Is it the "Jade Pavilion Spring?"
(Night after night, a full house of faces biting watermelon seeds.)

"Oh! Woe. . ."
With her hands locked in the stocks.

People gossiped,
In Chamus, she once lived with a White Russian officer.

Quite a sad tune,
The curse of every woman in every city.

For Ch'iao

This is the way I always like you to sit,
Hair loose, playing a little Debussy.
On the broken burdocks,
On the clouds in the river,
The azure is in Han blue,
And Christ is back in his gentle past.
In the distant watermill, birds chirp
Of time, when it is close to May.

(May they cheer to their own shamrocks)

A lifetime is such a long, long time,
Even some kind of a curse lingers on and on
In the pipes and flutes,

But to think of him from dawn to dusk,
Just to think of him is such a beautiful thing.

Thinking, living, occasionally smiling,
Not too happy, nor too unhappy,
Something flies above your head;
Perhaps, there is nothing.

Pretty straws are always bundled in the field,
He always kisses where he likes.
Have you seen showers sprinkle wet the grass and leaves?
To be grass, or leaves,
Or to be showers
Is all up to you.

(May they cheer to their own shamrocks)

Afternoons, she likes to recite "Every sound, Lentemente,"
Manicuring, sitting, drinking tea.
A lifetime is such a long, long time,
On the forehead of past years,
In fatigue words.
A lifetime is such a long, long time.
Under the beating of a song,
In remorse.

No one will ever say things like this,
Such things will confuse me,
Make me lost, far away,
Far, far away.

Translator's note: "Every sound, Lentemente" is a tune pattern of poetry in irregular meter, written in the Sung Dynasty. Of all the tunes composed with this pattern, the most prevalent song was the one composed by the classical woman poet, Li Ch'ing-chao (1081–1150).

Red Corns

The wind blew in the reign of Hsuan-t'ung,
Blowing on the string of red corns.

It was hung beneath the eaves
As though the whole north,
The sadness of the whole north, hung there.

As in some truant afternoons
When snow had chilled the private tutor's punishing ruler,
And my cousin's donkey was tied to the mulberry tree.

Or, like the time they played their pipes
Amidst the murmurs of Taoist monks;
Grandfather's spirit had not returned from the capital.

Or, like an insect kept in the cotton-padded jacket,
A bit of loneliness, a bit of warmth,
Such as when we were rolling copper rings over the knoll
And I saw grandma's distant barley fields,
And cried.

This was the string of red corns.
Hung beneath the eaves for a long while
In the wind of the Hsuan-t'ung reign.

Nobody knows the way red corns were hung,
Nor their colors;
Not my southern daughters,
Nor Verlaine.

Now, I have become old.
Under the eaves of memory,
Red corns were hung;
The wind of 1958 is blowing,
Red corns were hung.

Translator's note: Hsuan-t'ung was the last emperor of the Manchu Dynasty, who reigned
for the brief period 1908–1912 before he was overthrown by the Republican government
of China.

A Common Song

Over the barbed wire is the elementary school;
Further away, the sawmill,
Next door, Aunt Sue's vegetable garden
Growing lettuce and corns;
Left of the three maples, there is something else.
Further down is the post office, the tennis court,
And straight down west is the bus depot.
As for clouds, they float over
The clothes on the clothesline.
And sadness, it may be hidden somewhere near the railroad.
It is always like this,
May has come,
We take everything quietly.

A quarter to six, a caravan of trucks drive by
Under the bridge mound;
The river ties a pretty knot and flows away;
Grass starts its journey to invade the distant cemetery
But the dead never browse.
The main event is
Over the terrace: A boy eats a peach.
May has come,
No matter where eternity resides,
We take everything quietly, without noise.

Yip Wai-lim (1937–   )

Since China broke up and developed into two divergent patterns of culture, Hong Kong has become a center of impact in the clash between these cultures. As a British colony, Hong Kong does not have a particular Chinese consciousness. Thus, for the more than ninety percent of Hong Kong's residents who are Chinese, the search for cultural roots seems an inevitably long and painful process. Like many youths whose parents moved in the early 1950s from the mainland to Hong Kong, Yip Wai-lim finished his high school in Hong Kong. Unlike many of those same youths who went to the British Commonwealth for further education, however, Yip was among the very few poets to go to Taiwan for a college education. He studied at the National Taiwan University in 1955, when Pai Hsien-yung and his *Modern Literature* associates were actively promoting modernism in Taiwan. Yip soon became one of the active members of the group and a regular voice on the journal.

Yip actively promoted modernist poetry in Taiwan. His introduction of modern European and American poetry and poetic theories generated a tremendous influence, particularly among the *Epoch* poets with whom he was associated. His poetry is often imbued with ambiguity and its syntax often dislocated, but Yip is a capable lyricist who can subtly delineate his feelings. Yip received his doctorate in comparative literature from Princeton University in 1967 and currently teaches at the University of California at San Diego.

Poetry:

Fugue, 1963
Sad Crossing, 1969

Brink of Awakening, 1971
Legend of the Wildflowers, 1975
Sound of Blooming, 1977
Legend of the Pine Birds, 1982
Fleeting Travels, 1982

The Story of Wildflowers

Wildflowers,
After the burning artillery subsides,
Vigorously bloom.
Spring rains
Irrigate blood and hatred.
Roots of hope
Cry in the debris of a dilapidated town,
Echoing vaguely.
Pains and sorrows
Are the tilled soil,
Cultivated in the monsoon.
Over the slope,
"The wildflowers are fiery red!"
Songs roll up the hill
Through wave after wave of wheat.

Many years later,
The village old man
Sits on a stony stool under the banyan tree,
And narrates in various styles:
"Guns and cannons are drastic changes of weather!"
"Grudge and hatred are needed for the plot!"
With his southern accent he sings slowly,
Turning the drastic gun battles
Into crystal crispy tunes.
The audience is attentive,

Sheds tears of mourning
For both sides' dead;
All seem to say,
"Oh! Death is after all
An irreversible fact!"
Moreover,
"Guns and cannons are drastic changes of weather!"
"Grudge and hatred are needed for the plot!"
The audience is moved and agitated,
Sways with the southern singing.
Only I, looking on without pretense,
Run the entire way to the hilltop,
To pluck a large bundle of wildflowers,
To hold them to my bosom like a bleeding soldier,
And stand still on top of the hill:
"The wildflowers are fiery red!"
Songs roll up the hill, rushing through
Wave upon wave of wheat.

Waking Up: A Song

Upon distant water, rain falls.
                  Waking up:
Gray doves pecking? Or
Nails being driven into boxes or a
Downpour in the junkyard
Caught in first daylight?
Wind
Rushing 60 or 70
m.p.h.
Cut into confusion.
Ticker tapes.
A full sky.

The kitchen utensils, shoes, clothes
Weigh heavily down
Like rainclouds.
          Discarding the kettle
The faucet and coverings
Of cares from the body,
I clamber up my hair to
The river. Fetch water. Make tea.
Walls spiral upward—
Overheard ringing of the bells of fire engines.
(Clear and cool, river's water!)
Departs a new ship from the yard. Away, deserted iron-pieces!
(The river's waters brim as fragrantly as flower-tea!)
Chrysanthemums about the nursery
Darkly fill the hems of cloth,
Although wind
Rushing 60 or 70
m.p.h.
Cuts into the confusion.

Must go to the limpid river
To fetch water, of chrysanthemum fragrance
To let hair, of a chrysanthemum smell
Spread over the river's face
As it now spreads over
The body uncovered of cares.
Must go, a skirt turning toward
The rimless—
Seen and unseen in the mist
Holding the river's water—
The rimless skylight. . .

Day in day out
Keeping vigil by the dark river.
Flowers, white, dazzling
Flowers, enormous
Drift beyond
The rimless skylight.

At the gorge on the beach
A seagull swoops down to catch
A fish thrown in the air
By the seagull feeder

      Waking up:

The rain falls
Upon distant waters.

The Voice of Blooming

Are these the unheard voices:
The voice of falling,
The voice of shining,
The voice of blooming?
Your rising
Overlaps sea with sky;
Makes the clouds
Among white bursting currents
To disturb ancient holocausts.
Where ends a song?
At the mountain range's greenness?
In the yellow bird's path?
In the sea gulls' flight?
When all colors are found in one,
When every voice ceases at your beauty,
Distant cities disperse, and
Cliffs sink:
An enormous flapping in the empty, plain, stony face
Examines how knowledge does grow.

Amidst flowers: What disturbance
Interprets the universe?
With so many door knobs
Leading to courtyards and pavilions. . .

A stunning season
In the fierceness of your rising:
Oh, don't let rivers
Or forests,
Nor the villages
Flush away;
Don't let the watchtower fevor of frontier guards
Dissolve into
The voice of falling,
The voice of shining,
The voice of blooming;
Perhaps everything becomes a woodcutter's path
Among tiny,
Invading clouds. . . .

From Old Mrs. Mo of Heng Yang: A Letter to My Son, Lo Fu

Like a drifter returning after thirty-one years,
When your letter finally arrived at Swallow Ridge,
The Gentleman Castle of Heng Yang,
All were amazed at the revival of this old address.
Sad, disastrous years
Like rumbling tides, echoed.
Everyone talked:
An old friend, a wandering son,
Returns. Has his hair frosted?
How to recall those wrinkled childhood years?
To me, your voice remains as loud as adolescence,
Breaking away time and space
With: Mother, mother!
Just so rashly, yet so lovingly, as before.
Maybe you've dreamt
How I wish for our reunion,

By the streaming Hsiang River filling the spacious Lake Tung T'ing,
Where we talk over things of ten years,
Twenty, or thirty,
Things we know or not—
How to add to my silence
At your leaving?
Out of the mountain city, blood remains unthawed;
In the misty rain, sobs do choke,
And they said
When illness approaches death, hope remains,
When life overcomes death, illness departs—
Maxims so unimportant, now.
You did come, but not to ask:
Have the winter plum flowers bloomed?
Instead: How is mother?
    Father?
Stuttering like a clumsy country lad.
But at your speaking,
My barren heart brimmed,
New tears rushed from the wells of my eyes,
Erasing those tracked in all, other years.
Son, I am happy.
I passed through death, and live.
Deaths are old acquaintances,
Political storms, my old arthritis.
Time and space
Began again with your call;
Your yearning call
Revived death, but also relief.
I trembled and was chilled,
My head ached,
Eyesight dimmed,
Lower limbs lost feeling;
I suffered a stroke, vertigo, anemia, afflictions
Folding down like huge, dark wings
To beat upon the happy years of your childhood.
Your strong yearning call has rekindled enough of me

To go peacefully.
Son, forgive me,
Understand, I am old-fashioned,
In my own past;
Nostalgic,
In my old age.
Don't let them modernly cremate me,
I love my soil
As I guarded your newborn fecund whiteness.
Living, we have clothes;
Can we die and not have coffins?
Yes, a selfish idea, unscientific, un-Marxist,
Son, but all of you, understand,
Don't let them. . .
Don't let them. . .
When your branches glitter against a blue sky,
My root will, merged with the engendering soil, be
Filled with blessings, silently.

The Resounding Wall

A secret hidden thirty years
Now, as with new lovers,
Let me outpour
On the resounding wall.

Tomorrow, I die;
My cold-blooded hands,
My shame and accustomed violence,
All to expire within my petrified body,
Bringing with suspicion, hatred,
A fixed defense mechanism
Accompanying my fatigue
(Oh! Formulaic fatigues).

One word separates our two worlds.
My love, so rare
To see you on such a passionate night,
The eve of death.
As I wander under an unfamiliar moon,
Something of a feeling—
"Fragrant mists wetting the cloudy sideburns"—
A feeling of long desertion,
Like angry waves pounding the shore,
Rushes my petrified eyes and nose,
Ears and skin,
Reaching that deep, forgotten heart,
And loosing my tears.
Forgive this sudden deluge of emotion,
But this is the first time, the very first,
That I discover how deeply in love with you I am,
That I loved you:
When I wielded the sword in bloody hands,
Disgraced you with dirty slangs,
Consorted with others to deface you,
Created rushing waves of hatred, people to drown our homeland.
And I tell you that I love you dearly?
All is transient!
Tomorrow, I die,
But today beg—not your deep love
Which I do not deserve—
But that you cultivate my sprout of love rekindled;
Maybe one day
More people will come to the resounding wall,
Like you under the moon tonight,
And will listen to a last humble pledge of love before death.

Chou Meng-tieh (1920–   )

Anyone familiar with the streets of Taipei in the past twenty years will certainly know Wu Ch'ang Street. If also familiar with the Taipei literary scene, he will know that in the first section of Wu Ch'ang Street is the Star Cafe, a common meeting place for artists and writers. And, if familiar with modern poetry, he will know that underneath the verandah of the Star Cafe—on the front porch of the Hung Da Tea Shop, to be exact— is a small book stand. He who once sold books at that stand is our poet, Chou Meng-tieh. In 1981, Chou suffered a severe hemorrhage of his ulcerous stomach and, after hospitalization, had to quit the bookvending business. Since then, the location of No. 5 in the First Section of Wu Ch'and Street has become a historical site for modern poetry in Taiwan.

Chou came with the army to Taiwan when he was 28 years old; seven years later, he left the army to sell books on Wu Ch'ang Street. Chou Meng-tieh is his penname. *Meng-tieh,* dreaming the butterfly, is reminiscent of the free wandering and transformation of the philosopher Chuang Chou. The 1959 publication of his first volume of poetry, *The Solitary Kingdom,* made him a lonely emperor of his poetic kingdom. In 1965, he published *Herb of the Reincarnated Soul,* which merged his mundane world with the mythical realms of Buddhism and Taoism. For many years he studied Buddhism and engaged in metaphysical thought; his poetry reflects his philosophical interpretations of the past, present, and future. His terse and lyrical diction is similar to that found consistently in the Blue Stars poets, with whose activities Chou was closely associated. Yet we know that, behind the seeming indifference of Zen or the detachment of Tao, there is a poet's heart engaged in the fiery world of human affairs. Chou's poems often reflect complex emotions, and his unbending romantic spirit has made him a poet of powerful persuasion, rather than merely a spokesman for particular philosophical or religious ideologies.

Poetry:

The Solitary Kingdom, 1959
Herb of the Reincarnated Soul, 1965, 1977

Impressions at the Vulture Peak

In the assemblage of the Vulture Peak, Buddha took the flower and turned it in his fingers, but said nothing. Everyone in the assembly was mystified, except Mahakashyapa, whose smile acknowledged the Buddha's sign-teaching, and who was thereupon entrusted with the handing down of this truth to posterity. Thus the transmission went on from generation to generation, without verbal preaching or written scripture.

From *Records of the Moon Pointing*

One, two, three. . . nine, then, and more
Snowflakes flutter into the plum flowers and disappear.

From *"On Snow"—Anonymous*

Disappearing in a glimpse!
This snowflake, so deeply chilled,
Let a hand, so soft as if boneless,
Casually lift it.

The clap of thunder and flash of lightning!
But the silence after,
What a lovely hour!

The man, so ordinary,
The man picks up another smile with a smile,
Casually.

Flakes of Auspicious Snow Fall Here

All flow from the Dharma Realm to the Dharma Realm.
From the *Hua-yen* Sutra

When it comes to coldness, this is the pinnacle,
The beginning of an end,
The origin.

We all came the way of coldness!
(Such a thin Divide)
And hurriedly rush to a different world,
So removed from our homeland;
Where will these hurried travelers stay, or go?
In darkness, the origin of snow
Requires our use
Of another Eye.
Born in coldness, raised in coldness,
Ruined in coldness, and there chilled.
The higher mountain means the smaller moon,
The thicker clouds, a deeper sorrow;
And as for a sunset, only an inch is left.

A golden arm supports your arm;
Joyful feet guide your steps,
Pining travelers!
Dispense with your alms bowls;
Forget the wind and the flag, and
Look for your footprints.

Do you yet recall those rugged yesterdays?
The straw hat, the raincoat
And sandals bought with hardship money?
All are labors lost!
The road is to be traveled,
But once upon it, the way is far.
When is the day of returning?
Where is the full sky of magpies fluttering toward you?

"Illiterate winds devastate flower bushes."
There is no stopping spring.
Listen! Pines over the peaks,
Pine waves over the pines.
Look!
On the distant rain-laden grass,
Smiles and tear-tracks of ancient history.

Thirteen White Chrysanthemums

On September 13, 1977, I was given the wisdom beads from
the Shan-tao Temple. Upon returning, a bunch of chrysanthe-
mums was left on the right of my rattan chair at my bookstall.
The flowers were fragrant and resplendent, but I do not know
who left them. I brought them back to my small attic and put
them in a pitcher of water. Three days later, they died.
                                    Recorded on January 23, 1979

Never so much befuddled
Between my gain and loss.
Under an abrupt morning sun,
Amidst car noises and human shadows,
My thought turned white!

I shuddered at the number thirteen,
A number for wordless elegy.

A sudden fare-thee-well
Invaded my heart like poplars.
The stone pillar appeared to me a tomb,
The broken, mottled bookstall, a barren tomb slab!

Had my corpse disintegrated into
Gravels within the tomb?
Was it the fleeting return of my spirit wandering
From a thousand miles away, to ponder:
Whose are these flowers?
Like the soil with overnight moisture,
Where and who is the unknown faraway traveler
Bestowing this bunch, silent and fragrant?

Things beyond speech,
Karma long ago,
Be they buddha, drifter, words, or bone and flesh
Deep in misty clouds,
This person! She must have shared with me
Close and far, a union and separation;
But relationships are inseparable.
Once related, they sustain in the wheels of life.

I partake of the universe's feelings,
I partake of the maternal water and earth,
The paternal wind and sun.
I partake of you, chrysanthemums!
When grass sears, or frost deadens,
You bloom neither for one nor for everyone;
You, with sleepless eyes of autumn,
Multipetaled, multilayered,
The hearts of those who are dead you brighten
With your hosts of cold, flickering fires.

No butterfly appears in T'ao Ch'ien's poems;
Why commune with chrysanthemums?

Because among their sad tossings
Suddenly I find myself:
A drunk self, with or without wine,
A self weightless and without size
But jollifying, among the half-dry
Drooping tears of fragrance.

Huan Fu (Ch'en Ch'ien-wu) (1922–)

A senior member of the generation of "Bamboo Hat" poets, Huan Fu began writing poetry in Japanese during the final years of the Japanese annexation of Taiwan. Then he was silent for some time. More than ten years after Taiwan was returned to China, he resumed writing. His silence probably indicates an adjustment stage, during which he groped for a new mode of expression. From 1963 to 1974, he published five volumes of poetry, confirming his abundant creativity. His poetry mixes an artistic sensibility with social criticism; it delivers a strong and persuasive social message. His narrative poem, "The Wild Deer," for example, demonstrates a sensibility that depicts both the death of a wild deer and, symbolically, the death of mother nature.

Huan Fu also translates modern Japanese poetry, including the writings of Tamura Ryuichi.

Poetry:

In Thick Woods, 1963
Sleepless Eyes, 1965
The Wild Deer, 1969
Manuscript of Anatomy, 1974
The Bound Feet of Ma-Tsu, 1974
Safety Island, 1985

Flower

Give three flowers to a maiden: one on her hair, one on her breast, one on her shame. Then, she is very happy to be a woman—a dream she once had. In the dream, she feared bearing horrible fruits. She is afraid of fruits. Deep in her eyes afire with love, she refuses all fruits, which is a pronoun, a substitute of virtue for scandal.

But she does not dwell on the problem of fruit. She can put off a decision, can stop on the moment, before the climactic point. Then she takes off the last flower and becomes, once more, a clever but common girl.

She claims to be a stubborn woman, one who breaks half and half conservatism and liberalism, who falsifies the flower she is. But her speech isn't stubborn, is it. When in others' eyes she wishes to appear a good woman, she will break her silence with longwindedness; when she sees a submissive man moved by her long tongue, she fantasizes the bright eyes of three flowers. She dreams beautiful dreams, with the complete dedication of love.

A flower on her hair. A flower on her breast. A flower on. . . She again removes the last flower, reconstructing once again the entire universe.

The Wild Deer

Like many other shoulders, the shoulder of the wild deer has minute, long-enduring moles. Yellowish buddings of the bead-tree cover the deer's eyes. A yellowish evening approaches, but the stubborn, ancient sunset desires to reflect once again the virile youth of mountain peaks. The ranges of the Jade Mountain stand magnificent, sublime. But this time, this time the deer is not temporarily crouching. The fragile wild deer gazes at Jade Mountain, and is aware of the moles on its shoulder. One bursts gently into a crimson peony.

Blood gushes, using the speed of memory to educate the wild deer. A curtain of denoument lowering, the deer no longer considers the hunter's sharp arrowhead.

Quickly, the crimson sunset displays all remote memories; a usual concern, the taste of a silent, imminent death, disappears. Reminiscing becomes eternity. Hark! The ancestors of the Amei tribe once possessed seven suns, and seven suns really did scorch love of the yellow skins. Everyone sighed at the excessive authority, at the exploitation in the harvest of desires. This explains why the Amei ancestors went out in groups, forded rivers, took risks: to hunt down the suns. Blood again gushes out.

Rosy and innocent is the blooming peony. Now, there is only one sun. Now, only the indifferent wilderness possesses determination and affection. In stark and real indifference, blood spurts incessantly from the wild deer's trembling shoulder. The deer has not constructed curses, and the sore begins losing its pain. Scorching sunrays, which radiate the rise and fall of all endless troubles, now remotely rise and fall with legends.

The knoll where the wild deer crouches already is dark and silent. The beautiful, spacious woods forever, now, belong to the realm of death—the wild deer ponders again and again. Its pupils blur, and no longer reflect horrible faces encroaching on the wood, or the love of comrades vying for a ewe. Oh! Love! Love slumbers soundly in the fatigue of joy. Slumber. . . soundly. . . .

Lotus

Oh, please don't,
Don't stare.
I am from mud, anyway.

"Purity" exposes only my apparent vanity;
"Joy" is my bath in fountain sprays.

Through waterdrops rises a rainbow,
That little rainbow is the vanity I pursue;
When a rainbow disappears, so goes my world.
Perhaps, you may have known.

My matrix multiplies in mud;
At season's change, I wither
To return, eventually, to the mud.
Perhaps you may have known.

If you praise in me only a timely floral whiteness,
Please don't;
Oh, don't stare at me like that.

Don't, Don't

You don't have to give me your seat, lady;
The bus runs me rapidly and
Soon to my destination.
In this crowd
Think you that I, an old man,
Cannot hold on to his feet?

Don't, you don't have to pity.
Although I have arrived at old age,

I didn't earn it with effort;
Doing nothing
I could still come to be old and ugly.
Old age doesn't deserve respectable privilege.
Therefore, don't indulge me, don't.

My wrinkles do not request pity;
I have eaten history
And spit out conventions and morality.
To the degree of my wrinkles
I appear respectable.
But I know
That I am a debaucher
Who has not written a modern Red Chamber Dream.

Don't, don't tax me with your support;
In this crowd,
Within this rickety, public bus
Only if I can stand on my feet
Will contentment come.
Needing no other one to help me walking down,
I will soon reach my destination.

Lo Men (1928–   )

Lo Men is among the very few modern Chinese poets who persist in searching for the glory of poetry and art within the mind and the spirit. He is also among the very few who, despite a long creative life, remain unchanged on the course he chose for himself. He remains a romantic, who sees the meaning of existence in terms of powerful emotions. His *Undercurrent of the Ninth Day* and *Death Pagoda* demonstrate his effort to merge life with poetry and art. His poetic lines, which usually have a long, complex structure, partake of surrealism in their imagery and symbols, and push poetry to a deeper and wider sense of tragic vision.

Poetry:

Auora, 1958
Undercurrent of the Ninth Day, 1963
Death Pagoda, 1969
The Invisible Chair, 1975
Open Field, 1980
Selected Poems of Lo Men, 1985.

Watching the Sea

Swallowing every river there is,
You've drunken yourself into tidal waves.

Waves are petals,
The earth ought to be color-filled.
Waves are wings,
The sky ought to fly.
Waves fluctuate,
How could mountain-hearts not beat?
Waves come and go,
You swallow the setting sun, and
Spit a radiant morning one.

Always radiating tomorrows,
Always distant echoes of the orchestra,
Your hands stretch long, as rivers
Clutching at the summit snows and wildflowers,
Pulling in the scenery along your ways;
Scenery, though, is not the most beautiful or enduring;
Instead, the eternally
Blooming quietude on your forehead.

The inaudible, finally heard;
The invisible, seen;
The unreachable, here.
Vast and complete, you
Fill with sunlight, moonshine,
Wave-sounds and sail shadows.
Which horizon dare contain you?
When agitated and without control,
Your tempest and high waves
Strike, break against the cliff rocks, to
Release the sunlight and rivers.
Whatever you come across, you allow to go its way;
You lie undisturbed
And flow like the murmuring Styx
With March;
Quiet with waves, blooming flowers, and bird cries,
Coming and going, traceless.

Since beginning is end,
And end beginning,

Your coming and going
Is ceaseless running
To and fro from the horizon;
Indistinguishable in your silhouette
Is glistening dawn from slanting sunset.
Time itself, seeking your past and future,
Sees in your face an unnumbered clock,
Floating and rippling waves, misting rains,
But no reminiscence.
Should something have happened in you,
The storm will deliver it to the craggy shore
Where there are forms of years' beginnings.
If the mists can trace a beginning phase from
Pure waving and endless bellowing,
They are the heart of the watch,
And the heart of time and space.
Also, they are your heartbeats,
Collecting years, storms, rivers and streams,
To fill thousands of abysses,
And to burn into purple by ice and fire.
Still, layers of painted fog and night,
Nor deluges of the sun's paint,
Nor combing waves of combatant warriors,
Nor blood-soaked canons—
None change your stubborn, profound, gazing blue.
Even when—while distance has dispersed the smoke—
Drifting eyes turn back to look at the horizon,
Those eyes can't determine the nostalgia
Of your own gaze,
Or where any one of your wheels has rolled.

From a day of tedium
To misty dusk,
If you triumphantly return with the moon,
A starry night will crown you
With starlets all around.
Your kingly glamor and magnificence will

Reflect the lights, fireworks, and artillery fires
From half the sky.
You will climb the pinnacle of light
To rise into the next day's dawn.
All windows and doors will open to you,
The sky will be yours to roam,
The earth will be without boundary,
Rivers will flow to you,
Birds will fly to you,
Flowers will be fragrant for you,
Fruits will sweeten for you,
The scenery will seek you.
And—whether you sit, lie, or walk,
Or transform into mountain, plain, or river;
Whether you sleep or awaken—
Once a cloud draws near,
You will float beyond eternity.

The Tree and the Bird: A Duet

I.

A naked vastness forms your eyes;
Two rivers rush back to the first drop of water,
Calling me
And the original nature back.

All verticals begin with the tree;
All flights start with the bird's
Over rows of trees,
From density to darkness,
Then to coldness,
Embracing the entire forest.

Birds, one after another, take flight from the trees,
From thickness to vastness,
Then to emptiness,
Embracing the entire sky.

Trees which carry the forest all the way back,
When tired, lie on piles of golden leaves;
Birds which carry the sky all the way back,
When tired, sleep on piles of clouds.

II.

After the birds sleep,
The sky brews a spring day with colorful clouds;
After the trees sleep,
The forest waits for the golden current
To erupt from the mountains.

III.

The trees awake and
Rise high,
Extending their cones,
Stretching out like waves and ripples
Until their extended branches
Fill all space
Into the deep clouds.
Then, the bird awakes with a sudden cry,
Flies, fills its eyes with mountains and rivers,
And colors the sky again,
Making it beautiful once again.

IV.

The sky tackles the birds tightly,
The forest tackles the trees tightly;

Once they are released,
Hands in rivers will be forgotten,
Hand-lines in the sea will be forgotten,
Footprints upon the moon will be forgotten,
And forgotten, eyes in a night of stars.
Once they are released,
Rivers will flow beyond the universe,
Mountains will be placed into the void.

V.

From profound blackness
To vast whiteness,
From the dark forest
To the misty void;
The sun casts the tree, a spear
To hit the ground and stand erect—
An unreachably high flagpole:
The flight of birds transforms the sky into a magnificent flag
Waving in the wind.

Yung Tzu (1928–   )

Yung Tzu and Lo Men have been called the "Chinese Brownings." Also, Yung Tzu tends to complement, with her taste for the classical, Lo Men's pursuit of the modern. Yung Tzu's classicism is not a return to the past, however, or to the tradition of T'ang poetry, but is characterized by an elegant emotional restraint. She seldom allows her emotions to overpower her reason. Consequently, Yung Tzu composes both image and line with great care. Her themes are elegant, and she works meticulously to balance image with feeling. Yung Tzu was an early starter as a poet. Her *Blue Birds* was published in 1953.

Poetry:

Blue Birds, 1953
July in the South, 1961
Collected Poems, 1965
The Songs of Verna Lisa, 1969; later published under a separate
    title, *Snow Was My Childhood*
City of Fables, 1967
High Noon of the Flute and the Guitar, 1974
Bird of Paradise, 1977

Ch'ing-ming Nostalgia[1]

First, I need possession of the soil, the dwelling,
And a release from the pursuit of water and residence.

I also need to have walls that will resist water
Rushing in from all sides,
And to build my "workshop" warm and bright.
Then I can happily clean up
Heaps of trifling matters.
Simply because
My root is here,
My home is here.

In vain I envy my Taiwanese co-workers,
Born and raised in joy, here;
Their roots attached to their country's soil,
Without the need to bear the pain of separation,
Or the sadness for letters from home that never come.

Flowers bloom in the warm spring,
Dandelions drifting everywhere,
Relatives visit each other;
Purchasing a train ticket,
Taking leave of absence,
They step among other, old and new, friends and relatives.
They inquire about the living,
And mourn the dead.

Once, I too had high spirits on the road,
Coming from Taipei, via the North-South Route;
All the way down to the southern tip of the island,
T'ao Yuan, Hsin Chu,
Even Chu Nan, Chu Pei, Tainan, Kaoshiung, and P'in Tung;
But I have neither relatives nor home.
Returned to Taipei,
I still was homeless.

No garden trees, no birds,
No fences, no chrysanthemums in sunlight.
Under the rain and wind,
A lamb chasing the sun's dial
Passes the morning, then the dusk,
Passes the winter, then the summer.
My herding days are longer than Su Wu's,[2]

And yet the very longing of my heart for home
Is an undying spring!

Translator's notes:

1. *Ch'ing-ming* is the festival which falls around April 5, during the rainy season. On that day, people will take a trip, far or near, to visit the graves of relatives.

2. Su Wu was sent on an embassy by the Han emperor to the Tartars. He was detained by the Khan, but refused to surrender. He was then exiled to the North Sea, herding lambs for 19 years before returning to China.

The World of Verna Lisa

When objects diverge like tree branches,
The weedy woods fill with oblivion.

They try to peer into your world,
But hear only the pouring echoes of summer rain.

The misty silk curtain, light as tender flesh,
Covers your sorrow and fatigue.

(Noon is a wide mountain-shed, if you continue among
Numerous brambles waiting to be cleared.)

Seeing only butterfly dresses spreading a bright spring day,
You don't hear the troubled waters or see the cragged mountains,

And quivering landscape, quiet as an old flute,
And as chilly and indifferent as the temple bells.

No one knows the altitude of loneliness
        or profundity of lonely eyes,
Or the fatigue of a running river parted from the sea.

Verna Lisa, in this you ride alone
On bumpy roads, through the self, and vast loneliness.

Kuan Kuan (1930–   )

Kuan Kuan shares in his Chinese poetry the same innocence and playfulness that e. e. cummings showed in his insightful views of American life. Behind Kuan's comic mask is a face solemn and indifferent to the world's harshness. A biography he once wrote for himself follows:

> Kuan Kuan, originally known as Kuan Yun-lung, is a Chinese man, a Shangtung man, a Chiao-hsien man, a Ch'ing-tao man, and a Taipei man.
>
> He wrote poetry for 30 years, prose for 20; did calligraphy and painting for 18 years; drank for 31 years, smoked for 26, cursed for 40, and sang Peking opera for 35 years; he watched girls for 40 years and 7 months, believed in monsters and ghosts for 33 years, ate garlic for 38 years and 7 days, and loved someone secretly for 29 years and 28 days. He was married for 8 years, having 1 wife, 1 daughter, 1 son; 36 good buddies, 4,000 friends, ½ an enemy, 29 good teeth, slept pantless for a little more than 46 years, had 2,000 books, only 5 or 6 are good; had 1 hemorrhoid.
>
> He loved flowers, mountains, rivers, paintings, movies, women, kids, cats, spring, moon, night, bird songs; he also liked to cry, spit, and be eccentric. . .

Poetry:

The Barren Face, 1972
Selected Poems, 1986

Autobiography of a Sloppy Sluggard

Elementary school for six years,
Three years in junior high, three in senior high,
Four years college,
Two years each: M.A. and Ph.D.
Thank heavens I didn't endure all these.
Five times in love,
Two lovers, one wife, and three kids.
A few foes, two or three buddies, a handful of relatives.
A soldier for some years, on payroll for a few, but never fought a
     war.
In battlefields of life
A few times won little, a few times made truces.
I have a long gown, several suits, and several pairs of jeans.
I smoke a pipe, drink two cups of tea, eat three bowls of rice,
     and sleep on a wooden bed;
I am a born vegetarian.
I don't gamble, nor play chess;
A few torn books by my pillow side, I play silly.
I went through a few shocks, a few changes, and sickness.
In the sunset, I hold on to my knees and ponder:
In this nonsense how I spent my sixty years?
My life seems colorful, but it's goddamned ridiculous,
It's ridiculous, but it's goddamned wonderful.
When I look back at my unfinished works,
Ridiculous! Ridiculously wonderful!
Even a sword hanging on the wall
Wavers ridiculously in the evening breeze.
Even if as tasteless as the quintuply diluted tea in my hand,
I would like another cup,
Wonderfully or ridiculously.

Two Trunks

—In memory of my parents

I brought with me from home a bundle of clothes,
And put them at the bottom of a trunk;
Sometimes I took them out and put them under the sunlight;
After a while, I put them back in the trunk.
I don't want to wear them.
But I don't want to throw them away
(Though some are already molded).
It may be, I wish to save them;
It may be, I don't want them worn.
Let them rest, at the bottom of the trunk,
With dad's letters
(The clothes mom's hands made);
Sometimes, I took them out and put them under the sun.
It's a pity to throw them away,
It's a pity not to throw them away;
It's a pity to wear them.
It's a pity not to wear them.
(Dad's letters are so old, so crisp, upon touching, they'll disintegrate)

(As far as home town is concerned, it has become antique.)

Let the letters and clothes
Be bundled and put in the bottom of the trunk;
Dad and mom should sleep together, anyhow.
Would they be sleeping together?
Dying together?
Nobody knows.

(What is called hometown is a very old antique.)

There is another empty trunk
Lying beneath the bed;
Nothing is put in it.

It seems like something should be,
But what?

(Let me fold dad and mom, such and such way, and put them at
the bottom of the trunk.)

Fei Ma (1936–   )

In 1964, with the activities of poetry societies ebbing, a group of local Taiwanese poets formed the "Li" or "Bamboo Hat" Poetry Society, which eventually included three generations of poets. The senior generation, which wrote in Japanese and then in Chinese, includes Wu Yin-t'ao, Lin Heng-t'ai, Chin Lien, and Huan Fu. The middle generation includes Pai Ch'iu, Chao t'ien-yi, Tu Kuo-ch'ing, and others. The younger generation includes Cheng Hung-ming, Fu Min, Ch'en Ming-t'ai, and others. The efforts of these three generations have made the "Bamboo Hat" a symbol of the return to agrarian simplicity as well as the pursuit of artistic perfection in modern poetry.

Fei Ma belongs to the middle generation. He leans toward realism in poetry, and gives profound meaning to common objects and events. He tries to present poetry as a social phenomenon, and his intended audience is the masses rather than the elite. He uses fluently and clearly the language of the common people.

Poetry:

In the Wind City, 1974
Collected Poems, 1983
The White Horse, 1983
The Galloping Hoofs, 1986

A Drunkard

Walking a short lane
Into a bending,
Entwining
Sad intestine
Of a thousand miles;

Step on left,
Ten years passed,
Step on right,
Another ten years.

Oh, mother,
I am trying hard
To walk
Toward you.

A Typhoon Season

Every year at this time,
The woman in my body
For no reason
Starts a few squabbles.

Afterwards,
I always hear
Her gentle tongue
Licking my bleeding heart.

Television

A finger
Easily
Turns the world off.

But on the screen's slow fade,
There smoulders
A flicker of hatred,
Leading to an abrupt war,
Setting the Middle East aflame,
Vietnam aflame,
Every eager face aflame.

Night Flute

Guided by
The tightening, sighing wind
Of the bamboo grove,
A pair of sleepless eyes
Massage
The lane of the dark night.

Yellow River

Pouring
One sorrow, two sorrows,
A hundred, a million sorrows
All into this old river.

Let it muddy,
Let it deluge,
Let it change its course
Between midnight and dawn
On this spacious country,
Again and again.

One Thousand and One Arabian Nights

After hearing one story, he kills a wife;
After killing one wife, he hears another story.
Such Arabian Nights
No doubt were in my childhood mind.

There is always time to grow up.

Reciting the Koran, he kills a group of infidels;
After killing a group of infidels, he recites the Koran.
Such Arabian Nights
No doubt now are in my mind.

There is always time to grow up.

Tu Kuo-ch'ing (1941–   )

As a staunch *Li* (Bamboo Hat) poet and one of the originators of the *Li* poetry society, Tu Kuo-ch'ing immersed himself in the poetic traditions of T. S. Eliot, Baudelaire, Junzaburo Nishiwaki, and the classical Chinese T'ang poets. Tu was an English major in college, and his knowledge of other languages, particularly Japanese, in addition to his mother tongue, has allowed him to enrich himself with the current poetry scene in Japan and America. He was one of the earliest to introduce Eliot to Taiwan, and his efforts were rewarded with the publication of translated volumes of Eliot's poetry and criticism. Tu has also translated Baudelaire's *Les Fleurs du Mal* and Nishiwaki's *Poetics*. Thus, of the *Li* poets, Tu is perhaps the most academic, having studied in Japan and having completed his doctorate under the guidance of James Liu and Ueda Makoto at Stanford University. Tu has taught at the University of California at Santa Barbara since 1974, along with Pai Hsien-yung, a renowned novelist and Tu's long-time classmate from their college days in Taiwan, when they started the journal *Modern Literature*.

Poetry:

Frog Cries, 1963
The Isle and the Lake, 1965
Avalanche, 1972
Watching the Moon, 1979
Clouds of the Mind, 1983
Sacrificing for Beauty: A Sad Soul, 1986

St. Valentine

Who wants to be my lover?
I will offer her a small daffodil;
My heart is like the multi-layered stem,
My arms like long slender leaves of grass,
My ears like bugles hearing the spring wind,
My yawn, even, sounds like a bugle, scaring fishes away by the
   water's edge;
My shyness is white,
My inner desires are in a thick, yellowish, cup shape,
The fragrance is my sighs in a sleepless night.

To offer you a small daffodil—
But do you want to be my small lover?

The Isle and the Lake, No. 5

Every day, be with me,
Murmuring by my side,
Restless, flowing high,
Infiltrating my insides;
That existence
Coexisting, depending upon one another.

It diminishes me, but gradually
Expands my world,
Rippling with golden memories;
Sometimes, glamorous
As a broken mirror in loving-dying sunset;
Sometimes, it covers my shadow,
Turning away from the sunset, wailing.
Sometimes, it softly
Touches my wounded forehead
Where cracked soils start to fall.

I have no way to measure
My world; begin with the end of the clouds
Reaching the unfathomable sky.

Rats

Rat claws, rat claws, rat claws, rat, rat, claws, claws,
Only if trees have bark,
Corns have shells, corpses coffins,
Only if men have food

Rat claws, rat claws, rat claws, rat, rat, claws claws,
Only if roots are in the ground,
Supplies in the barn, bones in the dead body,
Only if we still live

In this earth, we protest,
Human beings vilify us as thieves.

In this earth, we accuse,
Human beings obstruct our freedom to cross the street,
They affect our joy in multiplying.

In this earth, if there were Mr. Democracy,
We would want to come out in the daylight
And compete the election with *homo sapiens*.

Dogs

Buttock against buttock,
It was the moment of quandary;

A bowl of cold water dispersed
Our casual springtime in a narrow lane.

Hairy mouth full of yellow shit,
Still licking on the sore spot,
Aye, our perfect match
And spring happiness
Drew the jealousy of that couple.

Boring days,
Go and bite a mouse in my mouth,
Fart just to vent my displeasure;
Let me lift my third leg, and
Slantingly irrigate that telephone pole by the road.

When night comes, I think of the day
When I came across her on the street;
Annoyed, I face moving shadows
By the narrow lane,
Fiercely barking.

Lan Ling (1946–   )

While a senior high school student in the Philippines, Lan Ling illuminated the Chinese literary world with the publication of *The Fourteen Starlights,* a collection of modern poems written by a teenager. Although she never visited Taiwan, her poems appeared regularly in such poetry journals as *Epoch Quarterly* and *Blue Star.* Her poems have a brisk rhythm, and present layers of meaning by borrowing scenic descriptions. The scenery in her poems, like the fluency of watercolors, is transparent but suggestive. She lived in Iowa City for a number of years, and recently moved to Cleveland.

Poetry:

The Fourteen Starlights, 1960
The Dew Way, 1964
The Talking Twigs, 1973

Approaching

I.

Circling, around a thousand sails and water,
A bird dips its shadow toward cold autumnal waves;

Its songs circle out
Away from itself;
It also demands that you circle out
From a boat where you are distressed by time,
And anxious shocks.

Circling, around a thousand black hairs and unhappy yesterdays,
A morning star enters into the
Water of your deep eyes;
At this moment, in your sudden enlightenment,
All the windows open up like rivers.

The touching heart is insufficient.
Only by waiting, you cannot spell out
The words of deep autumn.
Although they seem like stripes of light escaping.
The song you once sang for yourself
Flees into the widening view.

II.

Slowly falling, a heap of broken ashes attempts to tell us—the
beach will lie under a cold, nocturnal song; footsteps will lie in
the memories of tomorrow. It seems like yesterday, we worshiped
the passionflowers of our hearts, wishing to submerge our hands
in the graceful rhythm of words, wishing the murmuring river would
flow on our bodies, like veins. Then, the night withers

And days fall in a row of faraway drums, rising and falling.

We always ponder:

If one day, when images have no mutation of seasons, fire and
ice become old friends; and we, after being separated at the Great
Divide—we can still drink to each other, and talk about this poem.

Though the green mountains will have buried and covered us up
like our own foreheads.

III.

So close is the approaching,
Yet without sound.
The wind puts on the shadow,
And becomes naked, with a see-through dress.

A Car

This is a small pool of water after the morning rain,
Before a row of houses, kids have nosed their bikes into the deep
    azure;
Here, ivy creeping everywhere,
Leading the voyage of last night's stars,
And the boatman's dreams, quietly. . .
A fence before the street,
Where often the music of wind,
Choreographed by leaves of grass,
Passes by; this is a small city,
Far from nature, still, natural.
The new construction project's
Lamp-poles pale the scenery some,
But there remain people who feel
The coming of the bird season.
When peach and pear tree vie with their beauty,
Soft is the ground of spreading grass.
Above this small city is the clouds' window
Opening silently to a hundred thoughts.
Why, then, on such an afternoon,
Does a car speed by?
Raising a trail of blue-grey smoke,
Shaking gently the pool of water at a corner,

It may remind people of the sea,
With its news, its misty waves
That often bring tears to our eyes
During the quiet moments of hearts;
However, unlike the streetcar,
They do not obliterate with motor noise.

Conversing

When night comes, even shy stars
Will not blanket the silence
Of our naked, black eyes.

Here, the ancients buried deeply
A legend about a lock of hair;
We can go no further.
When dews are heavy,
We drink on the thin air's foam;
Although we've never been settled,
We once were happy like blind flower pollen;
Our every breath
Burned blind, blind words.

When night comes, we can only lie
Like two mirrors, reflecting
Each other's strange face,
Each having once loved
The other so dearly.

Listening to Red Maples
on an Empty Mountain

The hour cannot be more quiet and dark.
A little while we stand, in the wind,
Searching. A thousand drumbeats
Murmur in our ears;
Our dreamy winters steadily frost over.

The earth gropes
With a hundred branches
In the river of our deep eyes.
For the season,
If it were tomorrow,
Our loneliness should not be strange;
We would rather turn our fingers
Counting old names,
Remember one, forget the other.
We watch the mountain
Rise from its own echo.

Leaves lie inscribed on the rocks,
Saying, please forget all these!
The sound of earth is thin,
Where only ashes remain,
And of those, only late-comers!
And now, the mountain's forehead
Overflows with scarlet evening clouds, for
After all, we are not too late.

Wang Jun-hua (1941–   )

Like many young Chinese who drifted from overseas to China and then back overseas, Wang grew up in Malaysia and finished college in Taiwan. He received his doctorate from the University of Wisconsin and has taught at Nanyang University (now the National University of Singapore) since 1973. His earlier poems are characterized by a modernist treatment of themes and subject matter, blending the mystical East with the sensuous West. Since returning to Singapore, he is more interested in his cultural roots in the Southeast Asian milieu. A craftsman of imagery, Wang links one image to another by superimposition and intersection. He once experimented with Chinese by making poems out of the pictorial images of the ideograms.

Poetry:

The Sick Sun, 1966
Climax, 1970
In and Out, 1978
Rubber Trees, 1980
Beyond Symbols (English Translations) 1984

Landscape Philosophy

Above

Mountains far away,
   ridging, in slumber,
   no rocks.

Ancient trees
   verdant, and gray,
   no branches.

Green rivers,
   murmuring,
   no waves.

A man in the wilderness,
   cloud-watching,
   no eyes.

Middle

Tracks,
ending in bushes,

Streams,
lost in mists.

Shores,
broken by moors.

As the water split
a remote sail.

Below

Two mountains
   compress water
      into a creek.

Two lakes
    press the mountains
        back into cliffs.

Outdoor Collections

—Imitating Chia Tao

Buying a Tree

The monk carries a pine,
The pine carries a bird's nest,
The nest hides dark clouds of a thousand mountains,
The clouds come with the storm,
The storm spreads out a wilderness of ice and snow.

An Excursion

Weeds on an old wheel
    crawl into the deserted garden;
A seed on a broken tile
    grows into an old pine;
A lonesome walking shadow
    flickers in the pond.

Recluse

A distant pagoda
    is submerged in the autumn pool;
White clouds sojourn in the crane's nest,
    Fierce birds

dwell in deserted wells;
Autumn insects
crawl into the cracked steps;
An alert snake
drills into the core of the old *wu-t'ung;*
Footprints in the woods,
overlap the blue mountain shadows.

Out

Fireflies fly out from a dried wood,
A bird soars from a deserted well,
A musical stone; harmonized with the deep woods,
A stream runs from dark rocks,
A sail emerges from splashing tides
And hangs in full-blow autumnal colors.

Doors

Far down at the bottom of the spiritual creek
are the temple's opened doors;
When the cicada cries are profuse
the green shades are allowed
to enter the lute hall;
A recluse's thatched doors
are never closed,
But let mountain rains
freely in and out.

Chaos

River sands,
toe-tracks of homebound birds;
Ocean tides,
no signs of faraway sails;

Barren hills
　　big rocks left by the white clouds;
An old temple,
　　no kitchen smoke.

Metamorphosis

A lotus in the summer pond,
　　blooming in fiery fragrance;
A hundred roots in the autumn water,
　　all covered with mud.

Which Chapter

1.

After hurriedly burying all those who died,
And stepping over numerous names of the passed-away,
He returns to the boat cabin,
Hands still tainted by the soil of the Nanking cemetery;
Trembling again, he reads another obituary.

2.

"Let us go, else we won't catch the rest of the day."
He finally walks toward the brook reflecting a drifting sky.
Treading on the fall petals,
But not quite shoving off a woman's arms,
He steps over the wet tearful courtyard.

"Under the shadow of the Dragon Gate.
We were pushed back and forth by the crowd,

So many people
Chasing a tiny bit of so-called 'glory' on the city wall;
Again, again we were pushed down,
But the longing rope could not tie up the running sun."
He finishes;
There are roses all over the ground,
The bundle he'd held now trampled into the mud.

I wonder always whether this is heresy or prophecy,
Although a hundred lanterns light up the dark, stony city,
With drums and gongs beaten noisily,
Even the deaf lie awake at midnight.
But I wait until the day of the examination result,
And hear returning servants shout outside the garden gate
About his name being pasted on the wall of the Imperial City.

"I always knew and cursed
After his first birthday party.
Among the things he chose for himself
He picked a handful of cosmetic powders,
And put them in his mouth
And swallowed them down."

3.

"By kowtowing thrice, a sin is repented,
No more hesitation, or nightfall will close up the temple door."

On snowy ground, vast as a great white sheet,
He finally stands from nineteen years of kneeling,
Like a naked babe.

4.

When, beginning to understand,
He rushes after him,
He has already vanished with monk and priest.

He still pursues;
But monk and priest disappear beyond an empty horizon,
Leaving a mist of whiteness.

5.

Far away in the void come many happy tunes,
Behind him, his servant anxiously calls,
"Master, master. . . ."

Which Chapter—A Continuation

Following the wind and rain,
I become a recluse in Buddha's land
and wander in a narrow delta.

My dazed steps kick and disperse a mountain of clouds
Which blocked the causeway leading to the temple gate;
Toward the west
Lies the land of happiness for the floating world.

Three days and nights
Young servants hold torches
and search in the stony city.
They bang gongs, beat drums,
Loudly report the posting of my golden name on the examination
    wall;
Maidservants with long, hanging hair
Call for me along the cliff,
First calling my child's name, then my style, then my sobriquet;
But already I am lost
In the rising smoke of incense;
I sweep moonlight by the lotus pond,

Or meditate in the hours of the evening drum.
I have forgotten all my names
And the color of my hair.
The road I just passed
Is flooded with the tidal snow.
In this mist of whiteness
So empty am I, without even my shadow.
I see only a woman standing vainly by the Pond of Mercy,
Drooping her head, staring at a withered lotus;
A man peers endlessly at Greensickness Peak.
The Temple of Eternal Happiness is so high above that
The colorful balloon of death explodes
Even before reaching the pagoda's peak.

Translator's note: "Which Chapter" and its continuation were based on the novel *Story of the Stone* (sometimes called *The Dream of the Red Chamber*), in which the protagonist, Pao-yu, finally becomes a monk after being disillusioned by the transience of the mundane world of red dust. For reference, see chapter 120 of the novel.

Bricks

Setting down the bricks and her crane's-beak hoe,
She bends to the deserted, half-drenched tomb to wash her hands;
Her blood and dirt smudge the Ten Views of West Lake.

Stepping on the tombstone tablet inscriptions
She cautiously listens;
The unpredictable wind can so easily sweep
The barking of city dogs,
The crying of the child on her back
Into the center of the lake.

"When I had just dug through
and entered the home of darkness and bats,

He inauspiciously called me.
I said, then, let's find a few bricks
And hide them under our walls
To suppress the will-o'-the-wisp.
Thus we won't have to bring gold
And knock at the gangsters' door."

Before she exits the cemetery,
In the rumbling of the collapsed pagoda
She stumbles;
Bricks fall and break on the tombstone;
The muddied lake no longer nets
The floating silhouette of the Thunder Peak Pagoda;
The setting sun darkens and sinks;
A few startled crows fly into the dust of the citadel,
Where soldiers charge, and horses neigh
Following the bellowing tides of the rushing Ch'ien-t'ang River.

When thunder grasps her,
She still wishes to defend herself,
Saying, the troops fighting for territory
Will not reach the narrow path until tomorrow;
As for tonight, there will be no more earthquakes.

Translator's note: the Thunder Peak Pagoda was located near West Lake in Hanchou. It was related to a story of love between a white snake and a man. Ultimately, a Buddhist monk broke up the heterogeneous marriage and imprisoned the snake beneath the Thunder Peak Pagoda forever. The pagoda actually collapsed in 1924. People believed that Chinese women, out of superstition, would try to steal bricks from the pagoda, thinking they could ward off evil. Wang's poem suggests strongly that such a greedy and selfish superstition finally caused the pagoda to collapse.

Chang Ts'o (1943–   )

This poet, previously known as Ao Ao, was born in Macau and educated in Hong Kong, Taiwan, and the United States. His personal life as well as his lyrics are characterized by the search for a national and a personal identity, which is often lost in the tragic historical experiences of China. His poems reflect a tragic sense of life in which time obliterates personal experience and undermines its significance, leaving a final, total silence. Chang Ts'o has never given himself over to an empty, abstract consideration of life; instead, his subject is everyday life. With a lyrical and highly controlled language, he creates a poetic space in which human beings gain dignity in their struggle for meaning, despite the tragic conditions they face.

Chang Ts'o teaches comparative literature at the University of Southern California.

Poetry:

The Transition, 1966
Death Feelers, 1967
Bird Cries, 1972
Manuscript from Lo City, 1979
Sonnets of Errors, 1981
Grievance from the Double Jade Rings, 1984
The Drifter, 1986

Double Jade Ring Grievance

Nothing but innocent, stubborn stone, originally,
But ingenious designing,
Devout cutting and a craftsman's handling turned
A hard jade stone
Into an inseparable pair,
Tiny, delicate rings.
One ring rounds into the other,
In the theme of the eternal circle,
A complete past enters a complete future
Around the central void,
The double event of life
Commingled and confused.
Sorrow and joy,
Each with its own beginning and end.
The linked two rings are
Sorrow and joy; a perfect metaphor.
Jade is solid, constant,
Rings are without end;
The gentleman is as pure as jade
And his conviction is as unbroken as a ring.
But the rings' double design
Mimics irony and fate.
The rings touch each other
Only through a segment of jade flesh.
Like time contacting history,
And life is but that passage,
Once events occur, they are history.
One complete past linked to a complete future,
And the central void
Fills with innumerable, relentless regrets,
Unaccountable, broken sorrows.
There was a night
The double jade ring confirmed love;
There was a song
Exquisite and peerless, a line of which reads:

No one knows, except two hearts.
Another line:
A sharp sword severs the twin-branch in spring.
But the most desperate grievance
Is the pair of couplets in tearless lament:
"A muddy river has its clear days,
And black hair has its time to turn grey;
But as to secret departures and silent farewells,
Each lover is resolved to his fate, having no future plans to meet."
In life's mutations,
In the innumerable, unaccountable
Secret departures and silent farewells,
In the jingling of jade rings hitting each other,
And the murmurs of endless cravings and loneliness,
There is the suggestion of mutual regret and sympathy
Beyond history, beyond time.
But the double jade ring grievance
Is a fatal remorse
For history, for the present
Of people and things.

Empty Promises

> "Coming is an empty promise,
> Leaving is without any trace."
> —Li Shang-yin

Since I have given my whole life to you,
What else is there to regret and hope for?
Perhaps everything is an empty promise,
Like your arrival, abrupt but gentle,
As a breeze over my body, cooling, soothing,
Sweeping the young green fields of early spring.
The beginning is a widespread disturbance;

In the end, there are waves and waves
Of helpless restlessness.

Since this life of ours, I know, is over,
What is there to say of our next life?
Really, empty promises are empty,
Like the silence of your departure,
And my sudden waking from the dream.
I persist in searching for the scent of your hair on the pillows,
Among the blooming flowers of the bed sheets.
But in my own blooming, bitter smile
Is the taste of a ripe, heartbroken cherry.

Since both words and actions are empty, without trace,
Why would I wake and, still, turn to look at you,
And be filled with helpless joy?
I seem to have died,
Or suffered a horrendous disaster;
I wake and, upon your return, we look at each other,
You, vainly; I, wordless.
All right. Everything is like a movie, you have promised me:
When you really wanted to go,
The show was already over.

Confused

"Only at that very moment,
My mind was all confused."
—Li Shang-yin

Such an easy phrase,
Such a touching word,
It will, in midnight remorse, even make you cry,
Or rush outdoors in early morn to
Confront the new spring in melting snow,
Coldly to glance at the world—

Just for love.
You are prepared to erase your life
For the sake of those very moments when
Flowers silently bloom,
Rivers abruptly bend,
Mountain ranges appear in shocking reflections,
Hands touch each other,
Foreheads tap gently together,
And eyes meet, to charm.
At last, you rashly give over your life,
One tedious and helpless
With moments confused and helpless.
Yes, one life have you,
Yet, have you one love to give,
To sing, To remember?
Yes, one death to die you have,
But do life and death only repeat a song,
Again and again, repeating one single theme?
Handfuls of heroic feelings have you,
But you have only a single choice of devotion.
Whatever happened, what you recall
In trauma or in intermittent sobs,
Those are the very moments, the innumerable confusions
When you have only duty to oblige.

Reliance

"The spring heart of Emperor Wang
Relies on the crying of the cuckoos."
—Li Shang-yin

In the solitude after midnight,
Can one find a way to pour out anger? Obsession?
Those in love now sleep;

They lean against each other, circling
One end of the dream to the other.
Those out of love, too, sleep,
And each tries underscoring
Another round dream of his own.
Between love and its absence
Is a spatial exhaustion,
Equal in its race with a sky that,
After extending hundreds of rivers and mountains,
Still is unending.

At sunrise
Is there a place for
A tearless face—but crying eyes?
Knowing that you still sleep
Having loved, or not yet having loved,
You now sleep.
We will meet
After you have loved, or after you have not loved,
Perhaps after you have wakened and showered,
Expecting another lover.
We meet, and we love, and
Fall into another spatial exhaustion
Like the breaking of an embroidered zither
With fifty, or less than half, of the broken strings,
Still an empty chamber of bewilderment
In its solitude.

How, in high noon, or upon what, would a long, helpless sigh
    rely?
After bird cries, after tears like blood,
Forever there are strange embraces,
Strange departures, and reunions.
After meeting and loving
Forever are the familiar suppers,
The intimacies, the old dreams.
And like the morning cry of a desperate cuckoo,
Love still fell on someone else, last evening.

Drinking Tea

It was said that
Should you want tea,
You follow the stony path, covered
With verdant moss;
Coming upon a drooping, thatched roof,
Stooping, and
Stepping high over the threshold
You enter amidst the thicket of bamboo
A cottage for tea.

It was also said,
You must wash your hands,
Cleanse your thoughts,
Release all worldly dust
To the murmuring waters of the bamboo tubes,
Until your mind is pure.
Accordingly,
Garments are of simple colors,
And some things must not be mentioned—
Money, religion,
In-laws, wars, gossip—
None have to do with the drinking of tea.

Since the tea cottage resides beyond worldliness,
You should know the marvels of *sabi* or *wabi*.
When you hold the bowl with both hands,
Tip your head back, and drain the tea,
You should learn the history of the tea bowl
And its high aesthetics.
As you converse,
Your intermittent surprises and compliments
Have to concern the bowl and its possessor,
Since among the tea bowls
Is the encounter of predecessor and successor.

"Such an old, simple Shino bowl,
The dense, dark spreading dots

Resemble the blue mountain after rain."
Such commentary is only the layman's,
Because, though in making and drinking tea
You may define the role of the host and his visitors,
And the levels of tea tastes,
Only the simple philosophy and aesthetics of the tea bowl
Can soothe the relation of the host and his guests.
A master once remarked:
"Be sure you know
That the tea ceremony, in essence,
Is simply
To boil water,
Make tea, and drink it."
Such a simple matter
Can warm winter and cool summer,
And can turn someone to insist strongly, romantically—
The red tinge on the bowl's rim
Recalls from early years, red lips.

The Legend of Tea

It was told that
When the monk awoke,
Like crisscrossing footprints
On deserted mountains and snowy hills,
Traces of his dream emerged before his very eyes.
Feeling repentant and restless,
He snipped the thick, sleep-tempting eyelashes
From his thick, bearded face.
Accordingly, in a single night,
Shrubs of bitter tea began to grow;
They can restrain the hot tempers of the secular man
And love-cravings of the religious monk.

But from a sip of tea, how can I fully taste
The first half of a spring night?
From the tiny broken floral pattern of a blue porcelain cup,
How can I trace the change of tea color and astringency?
How can I discover the dried, knitted thoughts
From the submerging and the surfacing tea leaves?

"While tea is still warm,
You have left."
Every time, you complained,
"The tea is still as thick
As your homeland nostalgia."
Each time, you also said,
"Tea was made only once, and you left;
The teapot and hot water
Remain our mountain vows, our ocean love."

The monk finally sighed.
Shrubs of tea
Would be pages of *koan,*
Turning all secular laymen and holy monks to ponder
Between tea and meal,
From morning bell to evening drum,
"You came all the way from the East,
What does that mean?
What does that mean?"

To the Hosts: A Reply

—For Takuro

After strenuous cultivation,
We may sit under a tree, drink tea,

And comment on the sparse seasonal cherries.
On the summer cherry which once blossomed with weeping
    flowers,
There is nothing to be blamed.
Having gone through adverse weather,
Having borne unto death their stubborn beauty,
The flowers have expressed their spring infatuations
With a cry:
Love and separation!

This is like the spew of crimson blood
Spat on the lone darkness of night.
That is why, my friend,
We will not trace our bedtime romance
Nor blame our lonely foreign exiles
For the bitter sufferings of a lonesome cherry.

That is why, my hostess,
Once you've made the chrysanthemum tea,
And hold the bowl to drink by the fireside,
Don't forget to recall the heroic suffering of a weeping tree.
The crackling flowers outside the window curtain
Are indeed exegeses attached to heroic feelings,
Sighings for traumatic sufferings.
That is why, my dear couple,
In this emotional age,
We use cherry for red lips;
In this age of belief,
We use falling petals for drifting years;
In this age of *yukoku*,
We use the movements of the sword,
For the answers of scholarly writings.

The Tears of Pearl[1]

I. The Sea Shell

That year, for the poet awakening from his slumber
With sunset outside the window like exotic poppies,
An illusory Orient still lingered in his dreamland—
Suddenly, like a flash of lightning
Flickering vividly before his eyes—
Mongolians, with bare, shiny foreheads,
Braids encircling their necks;
Endless prairies,
A far-reaching sky, dark and deep;
High grass, low clouds;
Strong bows clinging to the shoulders,
Arrows hung by horseside,
"In Xanadu did Kubla Khan
A stately pleasure-dome decree . . ."
A waning moon seeps in and floods a barren land,
A woman kneels in grief, wails
Wild and sad.
Like a murmuring stream was the poet's vivid imagination,
The sobbing water, like clinking meter with
Short and explosive vowels
And rapid and masculine rhymes,
Oh! Kubla Khan,
He finally hears from the sacred river—
His ancestors' prophecy of war!
Upon the clamoring tides,
Western hegemony spreads like seashells,
Devouring the virgin territories of the Orient—
Gold and silver, silk and spice, and tea;
Steel-clad warships with fierce guns and cannons
Sailed into harbors,
Oh! Those hungry seashells
Clipping off the seaweed in their way,

Devouring weaker sea creatures.
The Portuguese, with high noses and deep eyes,
Queer behavior and strange costumes;
Guns exploded like thunder,
Swords sharper than rays of light,
Cannons huge—
All filled the mountain and the sea;
Under the pretense of paying tribute, starting commerce,
They built houses, then barricades,
Forced slave trades;
Finally they settled down in the White Tide Bay in Macau.
Back in those days, in the island of Luson,
Mountains were rich with silver mines;
Even trees, they said, bore golden nuggets;
The Spanish, afraid of the Chinese spying on them,
In one night executed twenty-five thousand Chinese merchants
   and their families.
And in those years, the red-haired Dutch came,
First to take Pescadores, then Kinmen,
Finally to head east, to Taiwan,
And build the Chih Kan Citadel.
But the fiercest was the big clam, Great Britain,
Deep and calm, as in the poet's afternoon nap,
They burnt opium into soft, creamy plasters,
Made smoking pipes from bamboo;
Beside the lamps, they turned Chinese into opium smokers;
The crimson blood of the poppies
Stained the Chinese land in large patches,
Turning the sunset in Nanking more red;
By a pair of lean, trembling hands,
Hong Kong was given away in a split second.
Those were the years the clams hegemonized the seven seas,
Colorful as murals in the dome which the poet forgets in his dream;
Upon the churning waves
Are flags, a single eagle, with double eagles,
Flags in blue, flags in yellow,
Flags in stars and stripes, in Union Jack. . . .

II. The Pearl

What night is tonight,
When I have the pleasure of enjoying the evening woods with
  you?
It reminds me of the poet's scenic dream where—
That deep romantic chasm which slanted
Down the green hill, athwart a cedarn cover!
Such a view of antiquity,
Recalling the childhood years of old bunyan trees,
Starting with the Laurenso Cathedral,
Following the clinging ivy of the Governor's back garden,
Stretching out to the bay under a crescent moon, with
Those speckled white, rocky tie-breakers
(Still bravely extending themselves to the sea);
Crooked old trees,
Yellow, muddied water from the Pearl River,
The sun setting behind the sails of returning boats—
All seem to narrate the same history,
The same changing events,
The growing ages,
The passing years and months.
The only difference is the mutation of people!
Many of the young summer days
Were started from the small pavilion of the octagonal library;
There was the time we rode our bicycles under the scorching sun,
From South Bay to Black Sand Beach;
We turned around at the Ma-chu Temple,
Headed toward the Cathedral Hill;
There, we held each other's hand,
Jumped over the barrier, and faced the land across the river,
Shouting:
"Hi, China!"
But what westerners fear is only Kubla Khan,
His fluttering hair and braids,
His fierce eyes, like torches,
And strong liquor, scarlet as embers.

We are no more than mud and sand
At the bottom of the hill, where
A woman petrified into rock awaits the return of her husband;
We are trampled by horses,
Run over by guns and cannons;
Gradually we become shiny and smooth;
We take the Yaumati Ferry to offshore islands,
We take the hydrofoil boat,
We travel on electric trains,
We sit on the long, slippery subway benches,
Where outside, it is pitch dark;
And inside our minds, there is a blankness about our destiny;
We join the boy scouts,
Get promoted from tenderfoot to Queen's Scout;
We join the Royal Life-Guards Society,
We join the Saint John Ambulance,
We study carefully the Union Jack,
Determine from the design of criss-crossing lines
Which is thick, and which is thin;
Slowly, under the secretive nurturing of the mother clam,
We transform ourselves into glistening pearls,
and, occasionally, are proud of our worth.

III. The Tears

Under the crimson kapoh tree
A dark complexioned girl plays on a dulcimer
A somewhat Abyssinian tune,
Playing and singing,
"I'm told all oriental pearls
Are come from tears.
The tears of pearls come from
The midnight wailing of mermaids,
When they first lived like fish in the sea,
And weaved at their looms ceaselessly.
Now they have to live on the land

Spending their days selling cloth
And living under other people's shelters . . ."
She plays and weeps,
Water and land,
Country and home,
National feelings and personal freedom.
There is no suffering
So bad as to stay under someone else's shelter.
A broken country,
A fragile identity.
Determination has become the most luxurious right and request.
An absolute choice,
An absolute contradiction!
Absolute pearls,
Absolute tears!
Today, there will be no primitive myths
To send a legendary hero
Riding on a scarlet horse,
Using his mighty prowess
To save the refugees from disaster.
Today's pearls are from yesterday's tears,
Yesterday's tears are the eternal sorrows of the Chinese.
There is a kind of clam
Forever hiding in the greedy ocean of humanity;
There is a pearl, which
Once was born, would be destitute, was determined to be de-
    serted;
There is a tear
Dropping, pitying its own determined fate, silently
In a moonlit night,
At the corner of the ocean.

Translator's note: Hong Kong, a British colony, is called the Pearl of the Orient. It was leased to the British for a hundred years, and in 1997 the island will be returned to the Chinese.

Lin Huan-ch'ang (1939–   )

A founder and leading member of the Dragons Poetry Society, Lin Huan-ch'ang has spent more than fifteen years in search of a poetic style which fits his longing for a national form in Chinese poetry. Coming from an agrarian family in eastern Taiwan, Lin did not receive very much of a formal education after graduating from elementary school. His sentiments about his village prompted him to write poetry in a plain and sincere manner, which opened new possibilities for realist poetry in Taiwan. In recent years he has spent more time and effort writing children's literature, including poetry for children. In fact, since 1976, Lin has published six volumes of poetry for children.

Poetry:

First Collection of a Cloud Shepherd, 1967
Turtledoves and Snares, 1969
Journey, 1972
Dreams of Childhood, 1976
Little Sister's Red Shoes, 1976
Little Stream Has a Song, 1979
Bad Squirrel, 1982
Holding Spring's Hand, 1982
An Elephant and Its Little Friends, 1983
Trees by the Highway, 1983
Confession of Reality, 1985

The Beginning of the Day

What shall I tell you?
Morning is the happy hour—
For work.

We'll all awaken
At this hour;
Sunlight, opened windows,
And the melodious cries of birds.

But do you know
This is the day's beginning?
Work, work,
Work is what I like;
Not something to long for,
Work itself is happiness.

What shall I tell you?
Flowers?
We're not here to enjoy;
If I tell you so, then
Shall it be a blooming
Or a withering flower?

Life is a journey;
What it reveals is truth.
"I'll speak,
But please do not test me."
Thus he spoke,
And I always heard,
A mind in supreme tranquility.

In the morning
I can tell you only—
Work!
This is the day's beginning.

Spring Morning

When birds
Start to call,
They seem to be
So far away;
In a short while
They appear
Flying to my window.
Moving their small, tiny beaks,
Pecking and playing in the sun's rays,
Which fall and form a golden-yellow silk window curtain.

The Doorway

I am a doorway of few words.
But how can I bear
You people coming in and out?
Furiously, I bit my lips, even my tongue;
Today, I'll speak out,
"Please, don't just walk in and out."

Hsin Mu (1943–   )

A leading member of the Dragons Poetry Society, Hsin Mu has brought into his poetry the harsh realities of society, making poetry once again a vehicle for confronting real life. His change from modernist to socially conscious poetry was definitely inspired by the new nationalistic awareness among the Dragon poets.

Poetry:

The Scattering Tree Feathers, 1971

The Second Winery

Like a rich has-been,
The Second Winery slantingly leans
Against the side of Chung Hsiao Road.
A big tobacco pipe in its mouth,
It smokes, from dusk to dawn.

Children play in the black snow.

Flight

We still have
To fly,
To rest, sometimes
To play,
To do the necessary.

Flying together may not be cheerful,
Flying alone may be bliss.

Yet, we still want to fly;
No need to be paired in sleep,
Or to become featherless.

The Meadow Upon the Mercy of Heaven

Except for heaven
Nothing helps.

This land
Is as bald as Old Third Uncle's head,
Bare, hairless.

But with open mouth,
Soundless.

Ch'iao Lin (1943–   )

Although Ch'iao Lin has often emphasized that his poems treat human themes, they are filled with surrealistic images demanding a sophisticated analysis. His poetic style, at least, has not been consistent with his themes. He has a solid control of cadence and rhythm in his poems, and the manipulation of rhythm is apparent in the following stanza from "The River is Still Running Like This":

> The river is still running   like this
> In childhood years,   like this,
> In juvenile years,   like this,
> In adolescence,   like this,
> Now, coming to middle age, like this.

Poetry:

The Face of Christ, 1972

Falling Leaves

Departing leaves,
Endearing leaves,
Silent leaves,
Cardiac leaves,
Tender leaves,

Blade leaves,
Hammer leaves,
Tearful leaves,
Individually withering
Leaves.

Pay the Bill

Dried bean-cake: $1.00,
Bok-choy: .50,
Fish: $2.00,
And a bowl of rice.

All over the streets,
Rain flowers compete,
Bloom and wither;
Shoes compete,
Walking.

Yes, one more Daikon soup,
And a bowl of rice.

Rain flowers flicker,
One supper follows another.

Oh, heaven,
Hand me the bill.

The Face of Christ

No tears
In my eyes,

No water
In my sweat,
No flesh
In my beard,
No breath
In my nostrils,
No words
In my mouth.

Wu Sheng (1944–   )

In 1975, together with Kuan Kuan, Wu Sheng received the Modern Chinese Poetry Award given by the Epoch Poetry Society. The Award Committee has commented on Wu Sheng as follows: "His poetic style is simple and real, natural and solid. He uses the rural language in a touching and sincere manner." Wu also stated, in his award speech entitled "I Would Rather Lose Myself in Simplicity and Clumsiness," that it is because he was not academically trained in literature and literary theories that his creativity has very little to do with academic practice. Instead, most of his writings borne from life experiences have to do with the sincerity of the hard-working peasantry.

Wu's simple poetic style is in fact a reaction to the overly decorative style of the academic modernists. He often describes himself as a common person who represents conscience, as opposed to the hypocrisy of modern intellectuals. He has affirmed his stance by insisting that, rather than using decorative, flowery gestures to impress people, he expresses himself truthfully, even at the risk of being thought to lack talent and depth. He further insists that, since he is a common man, whatever he himself feels churning in his heart tends to be universal and genuine.

A native of the central part of Taiwan, and a graduate of the Provincial Agricultural Institute in P'ing Tung, Wu Sheng returned to teach high school in his native town. There he has almost completely cut himself off from city life. He writes realistically, but his works are not as unstructured and plain as everyday language.

Poetry:

Soil, 1978
Impression of my Village, 1985
Telling the Children, 1985
Rocking in the Wind, 1985

Impressions of My Village

—A Preface

Long before long ago
The people in my village
First knew how to look up
At the village sky,
The nonchalant sky,
Indifferently dark or blue.

Long before long ago,
The mountain shadows stretching in
From the left of my village
Were a large gloomy ink-splash scroll,
Glued to the villagers' faces.

Long before long ago,
Generations of my forefathers dripped with salty sweat,
Raised and multiplied
Helpless descendants
In a land that would grow neither wealth,
Nor fame, nor miracles.

Elegy

Yes, I experienced youth—
Heady, hovering youth,
In the small village where I once lived.
I experienced youth's bewilderment;
Every forlorn beam of starlight knows.

Yes, I experienced springtime—
Fragrant spring,
In the small village where I once lived.
I experienced the mildewy smell of spring;
Every rotting petal knows.

Yes, I experienced love—
Intoxicating love,
In the small village where I once lived.
I experienced the agony of love;
Every sad gaze of yours knows.

Yes, I experienced singing—
Charming song.
In the small village where I once lived.
Once I seemed to hear my own dirge;
Every blade of the cemetery grass knows.

An Accident

How did a timid seedling ever
Sprout, bud, and become
A green sapling?
How did my reluctant cries protest
The fearful coming of the tiny me?
It was all just the most casual
Tiny little accident.

How did the green sapling ever
Branch, leaf, and flower
With unprepossessing fragrance?
How did my tiny talent,
After so many nights of torment,
Find outlet in a small poetry magazine?
It was all just the most casual
Tiny little accident.

How did that flower of unprepossessing fragrance ever
Bear its sour fruit?
How, after many a jolting storm
Did my tiny name
Acquire a pleasing touch of fame?
It was all just the most casual
Tiny little accident.

How did that sour fruit ever
Ripen, fall, and timidly
Sow its seed, grow once more into an old and hoary tree?
And how did the old tree sigh in the wind, and wither, and lose
    its sap
And utter a last choking cry of farewell?
How did someone learn of my disappearance
From some tiny obituary?
Oh! That too was just the most casual
Tiny little accident.

The Shop

Drinking, singing,
Finger-guessing, shouting,
Or sipping quietly, repeatedly sighing,
Or chatting at random, on things, people,
Spending these meaningless nights.

This is our shop,
A communication center,
An only refuge after dark;
All these years,
Forever crowded,
Forever desolate.

After all these years,
We, the unglorified ones,
Are just a group of images, blurred,
Wavering aimlessly in the air, in someone's hands.

Peanuts, another bag,
Rice wine, another glass,
Oh, televisions, cars,
Young men returning from the city
Don't reveal
Glamorous news far away.

We cross our legs, sit
On the wooden stools in the shop.
In our long lives dusty as the earth,
No matter how far we go,
We will be only a few short ox-cart roads
From the front of our shop.

The Rainy Season

Hey, smoke a cigarette,
Drink some wine,
Darn it, this kind of weather.

Hey, say some more things,
Tease the other gals,
Darn it, this kind of day.

Grumble and curse,
Calculate your pay upon the price index,
Darn it, this kind of life.

When it should have come, it didn't,
This rain, when it shouldn't fall,
It pours down forever.
Hey, rain, do as you will,
Darn it, we live anyway.

A Morning Scene

When the tiny birds
Are still sleeping with their songs
(Happy or not is of no concern)
Our village women
Are already sitting around the old well,
Washing briskly those old, worn-out rumors.

When the old sun
(Glorious or not is of no concern)
Has not yet climbed to the mountain top,
Our young boys in the village,
Summoned by their mothers,
Have left the houses in annoyance,
Without fairy tales, or toy dreams.

The old people in our village
Under the eaves
Recall memories trifling and blurred;
This is how they breathe the air
(Fresh or not is of no concern)
They see off our village men
Leading their cattle to walk on another endless journey,
One they've been on before.

Look, here's the morning scene in my village,
A beautiful picture, they once said.

Wild Grass

We are the proud wild plants,
Yes, we are the meek wild plants.

We receive silently the footstep tread upon us,
We receive silently shovels, sickles, hoes,
Scraping our descendants, freely,
But we multiply still.

Let goats, geese, cows come to eat,
Let them help themselves,
And the gamboling children close to us,
Let them come, run, roll over.

Neither sun, nor rain, nor breezes in spring
Nor anyone, can take over the rich soil.
There is no need to care for us.
Curse, despise, and shovel us away,
We are fecund still.

We are the meek, wild plants,
Yes, we are the proud ones.

Lo Ch'ing (1948–   )

Lo Ch'ing's works were once extolled as a new departure for modern Chinese poetry. The modernist influence on new poetry had come to a close in the 1970s, and Lo Ch'ing's appearance represented a new development, with new imagination and poetic structure. He can be looked upon as someone who, having been nurtured by modernism, escaped from that school's nihilistic attitudes. He is an imaginative poet capable of handling the most subtle imagery and contrived scenes. Since he is also a professional painter, he always has a prearranged set of ideas to express in an inventive manner. When modern poetry in Taiwan had begun to degenerate into rampant discursiveness, Lo Ch'ing's new approaches to form and content were an impetus to new poetic experimentation.

He was an English major, but received his master's degree in Comparative Literature from the University of Washington. Having grown up in an artistic Chinese milieu, he is able to combine aesthetically the West with the East, merging scenes and emotions from both worlds. At present, he teaches at the National Normal University in Taiwan.

Poetry:

Ways of Eating Watermelon, 1972
Legends of the Chinese Knight-errants, 1975
To Catch a Thief, 1977
The Invisible Artist, 1978
Rice Paddy Songs, 1981
A UFO Is Coming, 1984

Six Ways of Eating Watermelons

The 5th Way: The Consanguinity of Watermelons

No one would mistake a watermelon for a meteorite.
Star and melon, they are totally unconnected;
But earth is undeniably a heavenly body,
Watermelons and stars
Are undeniably consanguineous.

Not only are watermelons and the earth related
Like parent and child,
They also possess brotherly, sisterly feelings,
Like the moon and the sun,
The sun and us,
Us and the moon.

The 4th Way: The Origins of Watermelons

Evidently, we live on the face of the earth;
And they, evidently, live in their watermelon interior.
We rush to and fro, thick-skinned,
Trying to stay outside, digesting light
Into darkness with which to wrap ourselves,
Cold and craving warmth.

They mediate on Zen, motionless, concentrated.
Shaping inward darkness into
Substantial, calm passions;
Forever seeking self-fulfillment and growth.
Someday, inevitably, we'll be pushed to the earth's interior,
And eventually they'll burst through the watermelon face.

The 3rd Way: The Philosophy of Watermelons

The history of watermelon philosophy
Is shorter than the earth's, but longer than ours;

They practice the Three Don'ts:
See no evil, hear no evil, speak no evil.
They are Taoistically *wu-wei*,
And keep themselves to themselves.

They don't envy ova,
Nor do they despise chicken's eggs.
Watermelons are neither oviparous, nor viviparous,
And comprehend the principle
Of attaining life through death.
Consequently, watermelons are not threatened by invasion,
Nor do they fear
Death.

The 2nd Way: The Territory of Watermelons

If we crushed a watermelon,
It would be sheer
      jealousy.
Crushing a melon is equivalent to crushing a rounded night,
knocking down all the
      stars,
Crumbling a perfect
      universe.

And the outcome would only make us more jealous,
Would only clarify the relationship
Between meteorites and watermelon seeds,
The friendship between watermelon seeds and the universe.
They would only penetrate once again, more deeply,
   into our
   territory

The 1st Way:

EAT IT FIRST.

The Writing of the Character "Tree"

My younger brother and sister ran up to me,
Arguing, "How should we write the character 'tree'?"
How many strokes?
How difficult is it?"

Looking at my sister's
Round little mouth in her round little face,
I slightly rearranged the glistening braids by her mouth,
Picked up the wooden pencil that was handed me,
Thinking I'd say:
"First we must find a piece of good wood,
Carefully saw it, sand it, inch by inch,
Saw it square, sand the corners,
Build a tiny little village,
And not forget to sprinkle ten lovely little beans
In the middle."
I patted my younger brother's chubby legs,
Stroked his black hair,
Looked into his big, shining eyes,
Thinking I'd say:
"One stroke goes down like this."
But then I wanted to say,
"A hundred slanting strokes go like that."
And then,
"A big round blob will do."
I thought and I thought. In the end, I looked it up in
The textbook on the desk,
Studied the character for a long while,
And wrote down a most meticulous "tree,"
Saying, "It's very easy,
Just do it slowly and patiently,
Like writing 'brother' and 'sister,'
Altogether, sixteen strokes."

The Lone Swordsman

In childhood, I played with a wooden sword,
I chopped down spring flowers
And swore to be a hero;
In my youth, I used an iron sword,
I thrust it into the earth
And swore to be a dauntless warrior.

Now I have begun to know
Heroes often die in eagles' claws.
And warriors perish in menial hands;
Now I have begun to know,
Oaths need to be polished, in running waters;
Swords need to be practiced, in heavy snow!

In swordplay,
Changing the sword flowers into blood flowers is easy;
In snow,
Turning the blood flowers into sword flowers is easy;
In snow,
Changing the sword flowers into spring flowers is hard;
In blood,
Turning the spring flowers into sword flowers is hard.

Since I concentrate on swordsmanship
I understand the omnipresence of death,
And the continuity of life;
I observe the change of the universe
And watch the illusory void,
When falling leaves flutter
And delicate stamens spread their scents,
I know all the methods of swordplay.

In the life of a swordsman,
He strives to create a simple but powerful swordcraft,
The aim of his craft is to help
The growth of an infinite life in his killings;

The more he practices, the colder and more chilly his sword,
The more dexterous and warmer his hand,
The longer and thinner his hair and beard,
the shorter and more blunt his blade.

His hair and beard are as long as his patience,
His blade is as short as his life;
A short and fragile life
Is no longer sharp or glamorous,
No longer a reflection of broken blurry twisted images;
A wide and thick life
Will break through all illusions gradually
And strike at sensitive reality.

A man and a sword,
Moving, darting, leaping, ducking,
Reaching almost the emphatic realm of the "swords-man."
A no-action man with a no-action sword
Reaching finally the realm of "human mortality"
And "sword immortality."

The Sword of Li Ling

Hunan, Hubei, Taishan, Taiwan,
East and West of the River,
North and South of the Desert,
General Li! Hey you, Ling,
Show some guts, come out!

If good blades will not clash,
How can virtue be tested?
If heroes will not fight,
How can valour be told?

We met at first night-watch,
Talked swords at second,
At third, fought!
Wine bottles cracked, like high spirits,
Voices roared like biting winds;
Chairs tumbled, tables turned, doors banged ajar,
In a fierce tournament of minds.

Swords sliced the evening to drops of dew,
Scattering the ten-league mist,
Wills pierced the pine needles to cold stars,
Thrusting through the ten-layered forest;
Mist scattered, stars fell,
We saw each other more clearly
In each other's eyes.
Saw the faces after wine,
Dew and sweat;
Saw the long swords in our hands,
Blurred starlight and streaks of gore.

Saw the drifting swordsmen,
Hot-tempered, quick to kill.
In their sweat, warm tears,
In their blades, feelings;
Their swords sang like dragons,
They were tigers roaring,
The powerful thrusts they practiced with blood and sweat
Were given only to the initiate,
Tried only on the strong.

On that long foreign night, chilly and mysterious,
In the darkness where the road home lay beyond discovery,
We reached an understanding,
Showed the way with light of tears and blades.
Our unpredictable silence before sheathing swords
Roused the dawn.

The Story of Bitter Tea

"Rose leaf raspberry is actually a bitter tea"
—Shen Chien-shih, "Another Self Derision"

Looking for you everywhere, but unable to find you,
Perhaps the deep snow has covered hour tracks.

The first time I saw you,
You said, "Sit, sit,"
I looked up at you,
You said, "Have tea, have tea,"
I turned back and looked at you,
You said, "Come back soon."

I caress the worn-out table of stone,
Watch the tea turn from light to strong,
To astringent, to bitter,
Bringing the withered tea flower to fragrance,
To full bloom, like a fully bloomed snow flower
Spreading all over the perilous road,
Where I came and you left;
I hold the hot tea
And let its warmth slowly circulate around my body.

The day grows dark and cold,
You've been gone a long time;
Alone
I clumsily dip my hand into the cold tea, and
On a cold hard rock, inscribe a transparent "love,"
I silently see this "love," full of pure bitterness
Evaporate in my warm finger strokes,
Absorbed into the dark cold air.

Then I write another,
And another . . .
Each bears a different style,
Each differs in its evaporation and disappearance,

But the tea remains,
And you have not returned.

Perhaps, you have returned,
Perhaps, you didn't leave,
Perhaps, you are beside me
And I was unaware, or didn't think.
I have been unaware that you might have,
All this time, been in my hand . . .

A cup of cooled tea
Makes a dark cold me bubble.

Diary of a Prisoner

When my wife brings breakfast,
I see her miniature image, feeble, pale
In the red wedding ring on her finger
(Oh, my wife, once young, pretty, active
Now imprisoned in a red little ring, cold and hard).

When I devour my breakfast,
I see the broken image of my own gulping
In my yellowish watch
(Oh, I, once free, unattached,
Am now imprisoned in an old watch, unstopping).

When I squeeze onto the bus to work,
I see the twisted image, a dusty clamorous city,
In the mirror on the side
(Oh, the green trees and grass of my childhood play
Are now imprisoned in a mirror filmed over with dust).

Now, should I jump suddenly down from the bus
And rush back home;

Should I resolutely drop my watch
And grab my wife back to love;
Should we move back, lovers, to strangers, to childhood
(Oh, my innocent fairylike childhood—
But I always am imprisoned helplessly
In flesh daily needing breakfast).

Landscape in a Pot

I neatly paint spring water on the porcelain pot,
And put the pot steadily in summer mountains;
Then I paint the pot's landscape
Into a tiny autumn fan.

At this time
The snow scene not painted in the fan
Appears clearly on the porcelain pot.

Whatever gathers inside are
Of course
All the spring waters in the world.

A UFO Is Coming

UFO is coming,
Over on the highway;
Not star, not light, not firefly nor fire,
Nor anything to be identified.
It is an informal warning of the unknown.

To warn the human beings of the universe
To wisely use their knowledge, their intelligence
To research and understand
Relations among innumerable substances and nonsubstances.

Wu T'e-Liang (1952–   )

Among the younger poets, Wu is the one most concerned with reality, and deals in his poetry with real-life events. He looks at his surroundings with curiosity and bewilderment, yet beneath that lies a deep concern for life. When in high school in his native Hualien, on the east coast, Wu had already started painting and writing and, as both poet and painter, he is a sensitive observer. His imagery is colorful and dramatic. Instead of applying analytical and historical perspectives to criticize reality, he views reality and its people with acceptance and a caring heart. His long narrative poems on the dilemma of Taiwan high school graduates were in 1985 adopted into an insightful, satiric movie.

Poetry:

The Moon Festival, 1974
Atelier, 1978
The Meeting of the Swords, 1972 (copublished with Li Nan)
The Moon and the Sword, 1982
Heroes of the Junior High 8th Graders, 1984

Nostalgia

Sit,
Please sit down

And listen
To the ocean tides.

Let's presume we've arrived at the coast
With rice grain stalks above our heads,
Our light dimples
Heavy with sweet wine.
Someone assures us
We have fallen asleep.

Let's row on the watery moonlight
And wake all the fish.
The day has not yet dawned,
We're not fully awake,
Let's copy down our drunken words
And sing
All the way back.

Please sit
And listen to the ocean tides.
In case someone finds out
We've awakened on the quiet shore,
Please use all our letters home
To dry lightly our tears.

Sharpshooters

We wait for the moving mountains to break
And rise as memories, drifting.
In our moving viewfinder,
The mountains gradually become part of the sky.
Soil of a foreign land
Clings to our prone bodies, so cold,
Like the damp barrel of a gun
Sticking to our faces.

Plaster our bright blood with praise!
When we lie still in muddy trenches
Feeding our hunger with moonlight,
And when our thoughts fly southward,
Please use the tegument of turf above our heads
To conceal this restlessness of ours.

Hand gestures are our language
Beneath a sky absent of flying dove,
We silently wait for an incident;
No matter what happens,
We will not die in desperation.

Plant a black poppy in our enlarged pupils!
Let anticipation, from faraway mountains
Aim at us with the same posture,
Shoot down
This entire deposit of homesickness!

Night Guards

Our steel helmets
Serve to hold moonlight,
And our repeated perspiration,
In reachable fears,
To complete the presenting of arms.

Homesickness lies down in advancing darkness,
Our faces turn aside,
Meet the piercing wind,
While the other side of our faces
Fills out the tree shadows.

Boiling in our eyes
Are the farewell tears of mothers;

Their repeated advice gnaws our chapped lips.
After a volley of barking dogs
We abruptly wake.

The password already has become a time bomb,
Suspended vertically amid the sounds that pass;
As we march,
It becomes the perspiration expressed
From our tight buttocks.

On the cold concrete,
Our lonely shadows project
Into the sky at a thirty-degree angle;
Each step is difficult.

Bitten awake by the cold,
We lift our guns
And use the barrels to sweep away thoughts.
From this shooting position, in an endless night
We strafe the distance with our eyes,
Stand, and gradually transform ourselves
Into black pines.

Li Nan (1952–   )

Li Nan, a poet-painter like Lo Ch'ing and Wu Te-liang, started painting and writing in his high school days; the "2½ Mythology" is a long confessional poem he wrote as a senior in high school. His poems are filled with domestic warmth and ethics, touching his readers with sincerity and simplicity. Stressing a spontaneous outflow of emotions and a realistic portrayal of events, Li Nan adheres to a mimetic theory of poetry, of which he says, "Poetry writing is like photography; every poet is a camera, revealing in images all the objects he sees and feels. Once treated as literary objects, they become poetry." He now works at the *China Times*.

Poetry:

Meeting of the Swords, 1977 (copublished with Wu Te-liang)
In Memory of My Mother, 1978

Eight Poems For Children

—for I-fan

1. The Fifteenth Evening of the First Lunar Month

After the stars have disappeared,
The lonesome moon, with tearful eyes,
Searches for them everywhere.

The stars have sneaked down to the streets
Transformed into warm, cozy lanterns.
Joyfully they play with the children,
Hand in hand, in the world of humans.

2. Papa and Mama

Mama is a tree,
Papa's words a breeze
Blowing gently in mama's ears;
Mama often laughs aloud
Joyfully
Rustling in the breeze.

3. The Rooster

Conceiving of the universe as a big cookie,
The young rooster begins his journey;
He pecks at the earth,
Sometimes quite delicious;
But when he pecks upon his shadow,
His head droops sadly sideways.

4. The Dream

Father fell asleep one day,
Whistles blowing in his mouth.
There must be many dream-laden ships
In father's head.

5. The Dog

There is in the dog's mind
A secret he doesn't know how to hide;

Back and forth he runs outside the house,
Sometimes stopping to dig,
Sometimes sticking out his nose
Sniffing a while, carefully.
Somehow, unable to trust
His secret to a hole,
He gets up and again runs.

Tired, finally, he rests in the shade;
Imperceptibly, too, his secret dozes
Off in the gentle breeze.

6. The Breeze

In an invisible dress, the breeze
Tiptoes past the garden,
Steals a flower's fragrance.

The annoyed flower shakes her head—
Quivers loose a few leaves.

7. Fireflies

When mother was small,
She caught tiny fireflies in the yard.
I'm always seeing flickering fireflies in the room, too;
Wanting to catch them
I approach,
To discover, not fireflies, but
Father smoking on the sofa.

8. The Telephone

The telephone is a house without doors.
Father's friends sometimes stay inside,

Sometimes mother's friends.
They always ring for my parents.

I too have a phone, a toy
With my own friends inside,
Who never call me;
And they are never at home
When I try to call them.

Putting my Daughter to Bed

Very soon the day will darken;
Other children may be leaving
Their day's fatigue on toys,
But you must sleep now,
Like the red roadside dahlia you're so fond of,
Leaning its head softly on the night's breast.

Father will go out to electrify fish,
Will seek the tiny star-twinkling fish
In a river darker than night;
He will bend his back to
Grope among wavering water-reeds,
And make his living in a place no one likes.

Father fears the sharp-toothed water-snake
Suddenly twirling round his arm;
He also fears ghosts,
More horrible than darkness;
But most, father fears to walk into Ah Chen's dreams
Wearing perspiration and mud,
And the bitter tastes you so dislike.
This is why father carefully walks
To a place without stars and moon,

Moving further into muddied water, into dense reeds.
He will not block starlight,
Nor disturb the fish.

Good girl, do not fear
Cold, dark night,
Do not fear burnt candles.
Sleep well, quietly, and make a bright starlit dream.
If there were a spot of light, distant,
It would be your tired father
Sitting at midnight by the river,
In a faraway place, sleepless,
Lighting a cigarette.

A Letter from Home

The mailman brings
The concrete voice of mother;
I put away my faithful rifle
With greasy hands,
And begin picking from the white sheet
Pieces of words, dense as starlight;
They puzzle my tearful eyes, which once bid farewell.

Having folded the letter,
I put it into the pocket closest to my chest,
With many of my waking dreams.

My old clothes, no longer requested,
Must still be home,
Must be too small to wear,
Like a heart too tiny to contain so heavy a longing for home.

Tu Yeh (1953–   )

Although young, Tu Yeh has produced more than three hundred poems, which attests to his consistent creative energy. Moreover, they are of good quality, with striking imagery and dramatic content. Like Su Shao-lien, he writes prose as well as poetry, and his prose poems have made a unique contribution to this challenging genre.

Recently, Yu Yeh has undertaken a drastic change of style that marks a departure from his earlier poetry. Coming after *Glove and Love*, a modernist treatment of the classical past, the unfocused social consciousness in *The Grapes of Wrath* unfortunately lacks the poetic intensity Tu had achieved in earlier days. *The Eyes of Sunlight* is a collection of children's poems. Tu Yeh holds a master's degree in Chinese literature from Chinese Cultural University.

Poetry:

Glove and Love, 1979
The Eyes of Sunlight, 1982
The Grapes of Wrath, 1983

In Memory of My Forever-gone Nineteenth Year

In the beginning, I really did not know what was happening. Until I heard myself utter the first cry: Tu Yeh (Oh! Each happy echo was a sad, sad summons!) Then I rushed headlong into the heart of a dark cave. Later, I recalled, ". . . Darkness . . . was my beginning. . . ." Yet, I had already seen, had no time to intercept, so many, oh, so many Tu Yeh's rushing, pell-mell, out:

"For the Sake of Birth."

till all the Tu Yeh's
drown the barren hill
utterly.

Telephone Booth in the Rain

suddenly

a flash of thought strikes
O blood-dripping roses

wither

The Chrysanthemum and the Sword

"Would that in each and every life we could be husband and wife."
—Shen Fu

If I am the forlorn chrysanthemum awaiting execution, you are the sword, bearing sorrow. On a dark night in the cold desolation of the mountains, slowly you pierce my warm heart, and my yellow blood flows, drips, filters into the closely textured earth, roots, sprouts, forever without regrets. Finally, in deepest autumn, a chrysanthemum blooms whose past life you wounded, and once again on a dark night in the cold desolation of the mountains, on the plain where we keep tryst in each and every life, with tearful eyes, it waits again

> for you to be drawn from your scabbard.

> this is our last reunion; you will crack before my eyes, painfully vomit my yellow blood, and return all the blood
> to my former self
> the present chrysanthemum.

Spring Worm I

Having waited a long time
In your contrived nights,
I finally collapsed, a thousand miles away,
On the muddy, rainy groud;
Then, you slowly came toward me,
Sadly, regretfully
Spitting at me your feeble threads of silk,
Saying,
"Begin!"

Spring Worm II

I promised: a thousand poems;
I wearily spew silk under the lamp,

Far away, you impatiently wait.
All my poems, quite understanding,
All persist on a single theme:
In this life, we can't marry as husband and wife.
The trees in the world are sad;
Every seven years, when once we meet,
The clouds in the sky are happy.

In your letter, you whispered
Of reading with tears the nine-hundred-and-twentieth;
Trying to discuss
The problem of our future lives,
You finally asked
When the last poem was written, what it was about.

Far away, impatiently, you wait;
I wearily spew silk under the lamp.
When the light expires,
Crushed beneath endless piles of manuscripts,
I reply, softly:
My final death
Is the very last love poem.

Grievance I

When lonesome, I always stay in the moist courtyard,
Using your high tone to write my saddest poem—

   "If you are the falling of all sweet cherries,
   I am the return of desolate spring."

The Herdboy and the Weaver Girl

In the hour when leaves fall most abundantly, we still wait in our last high terrace. In that moment of darkness, we find each other in thick clouds of nowhere. Suddenly we think of, try to retain, with vigor, the forever-gone flower garden.

You must know, at that moment, the world's brightest star flashes through the back of my catastrophic, uncautious window. Lonesome and brief, it falls to the ground. Late on a windy night, I seem to hear your irresistible, tedious, soft sighing,

"But . . ."

Then you arise and gently fly over to me; so much like the flight across the cold, desolate Milky Way. At that time, you know only how to condense yourself into a pitiful, late-blooming star. Late on rainy nights, you deliberately ask me to come see you, flying down from my half-made window.

But don't you know, really, by doing so you've taken away all of our Seventh Night, our painful darkness, our joyful light?

Glove and Love

A printed English word quietly lies upon the desk,
"Glove."
I use it to ward off the chill of life.
The pair of dark leather gloves she left on the desk,
Eclipsing the first letter of the word,
Reveals another entire word,
"Love."

There is no phonetic alphabet,
We can read the word only in silence;
She picks up the gloves from the desk
And hides away love;
I quietly put them on my cold hands,
And let love completely hide in my gloves.

Su Shao-lien (1949–   )

A surrealistic poet, Su relies upon the complexity of modern language to reflect the mind's mysteries. Among the young poets, he most excels in developing poetic tension within a poem. Regarding the purity of poetry, he once proclaimed that "in today's society, it seems as if poetry could be meaningful only to the poets." He further complained that since an audience is accustomed to receiving prosaic meaning, and therefore seeks that meaning in a reading, poets should not criticize themselves for not finding larger audiences for their poetry. When, in a prosaic society, people's minds are prosaic, who can blame the poets for unpopularity?

Su has written a number of prose poems. His highly condensed thought and skillful use of metaphors successfully convey the despair, struggles, and hopes of modern man. To the surprise of the poetry circle, Su drastically changed his style in the early 1980s. Whereas he used to be devoted to long, narrative poetry with social intent, he is now heading toward the other extreme by making himself a social poet of native significance.

Poetry:

Collection of Lost Thoughts, 1978

A Piece of Seven-foot Cloth

Mother bought only a seven-foot piece of cloth. I regretted not having purchased it myself. I said, "Mother, seven feet is insufficient. We need eight feet." She replied, "Seven feet was enough last time. Have you grown taller?" I said nothing, just making mother conscious of her shortness.

Following old measurements, mother outlined my figure on the piece of cloth. With the scissors, she cut slowly. I slowly cried, "Oh! Please, cut me, open me, sew me, mend me . . . , and make me a man."

Frost on the Ground

Fluttering, twirling in air,
A single piece of reflective cellophane
Turns around the eaves, calls out the bats,
Turns around the thresholds, calls out the termites,
Turns around your body, calls out your legs,
Turns and comes to the front of the bed,
Dropping, falling into a ground of frost.
That is the moonlight, crying to go home.
You lean against the blood-red balustrade,
Watching the star forest absorb dreariness,
The concrete houses absorb emptiness,
The saber's song absorb remoteness;
Who doesn't wish to return?
I don't, since I am your past.
You look forward,
The moon is distant,
You already are cinders turned yellowish.

Carrying a candlestick lantern, you walk the bloody path
One step beneath the window;
You illuminate the sound of the flowers.
Three steps on the stairs,
You illuminate the lengthy corridor;
Five steps into the mirror
You illuminate the coldness of the face;
Seven steps to the bedside,
You illuminate, oh, a ground of frost.
That is the moonlight, crying to go home.
The clear sky is high,
Shadows blurry;
Which passage of time can be illuminated by candle tears?
Who does not wish to return?
I don't, since I am your present.
Where do you look?
The moon is distant,
You already are a pool of never evaporating watermarks.

You open an old, empty suitcase,
Bring it to the closet,
And put in mother's needles and threads;
You bring it to the ancestral altar,
Put in the cremated ashes of your brother,
And bring it to the attic,
To put in a few war-loving pigeons;
You bring it to the bed
And spill out a ground of frost.
That is the moon, crying to return.
The last time you left,
You lay on a stream of blood
Slantingly flowing into the Milky Way.
Who doesn't wish to return?
I don't, since I am your future.
You look back. The moon is far behind, you are the linen
Falling from the bed.

White Sheep Slope

A thousand wrinkles arise from the shape of Ta-tu Mountain; the cars riding in the wrinkles are like drops of sweat falling from my forehead. I touch my forehead, then begin to find myself with a high temperature. Dying. I look from the bottom of the mountain; there, a white sheep stares at me. Kneeling, the sheep is in tears. Grass stands high in the sky. Then, one after another, sheep start to be born. The whole slope of Ta-tu Mountain begins to stir and chew. In chewing, cars, one after another, drive into the bellies of thousands of sheep.

"Mother, you kneel and bear me; mother, how can I not kneel and be milked by you?" Kneeling down, oh! I look over from the bottom of the hill; there, a white sheep leads thousands of small sheep, walking into my belly.

Translator's note: Ta-tu Mountain is located in the central part of Taiwan. It's original name is Ta-tu (big belly, impregnated mountain). On the downward slope of the mountain there are situated many public cemeteries.

Mountain Barrier

All over the mountain,
Wild weeds everywhere
Devour birds and fowl;
I can hunt only myself with the gun.

Mountain climbers
Found me
Turned into a manure pile
In a diary.

Now the deserted mountain
Fades into people;
A chimney
Fallen at the bottom of the hill.

The gunshot sounds
Used to be nice,
But now the mountain barricades Taipei.
It's kind of sad.

Weeds

The water bridge by the river, the weeds have consumed;
Sunset is the weeds' tongue,
Twirling the sky to be swallowed.
You cannot ferry your name across,
Your hands are blades of grass, starving;
Brother, why does your body
Hide in my eyes?
I cry. How do you run from this world?
The wind begins to puff at the weeds,
Bending my brother's neck;
The swollen river rises slowly,
Holds me, says,
"I want to drink you!"
I close my eyes
And sink into the river.

The Blackbird

On the leanest black bough, the blackbird rests;
Leaves are his wings,

His wings are the black clouds of the sky;
Once they flap,
Leaves fall,
Clouds spread.
Under the tree lies my lost younger brother,
The spider weaving him an umbrella, and
A map to find his way home.
Because of him,
The spider falls into the soil of death.
Everywhere is my brother's face,
Gyrating up the tree, and
Rushing toward the blackbird
To become the face of the blackbird.
On the leanest black bough rests the blackbird;
In the year-rings, the sun expands.

A Little Girl's Show

No one introduces the show,
She chooses the soil—
And performs there:
She thanks a clump of wild grass, growing slowly to become the
    backdrop;
She thanks the ants, arranging in good order the rows of seats;
She thanks the moon, controlling skillfully the changes in light-
    ing;
She thanks the spring for her makeup;
She thanks the rivers, rushing down the mountain for her music;
She thanks the dragonfly, conducting with its tail;
She thanks the insects for making a full house;
Yet,
The only applause is from butterflies
    beating their wings.

Chiang Hsun (1947–   )

After enthusiastically learning for two decades about western literature, which flooded the Taiwanese literary scene in the 1950s, writers of the 1970s were awakened to a strong sense of nationalism, turning their eyes to the social reality of Taiwan. They were inspired by such incidents as the Fishing Island dispute, Taiwan's departure from the United Nations, Richard Nixon's visit to Peking, and the severance of Sino-Japanese diplomatic relations. Many poets felt an urgent need to return to Chinese cultural roots and reassess their Chinese identity. Chiang Hsun has emerged as a voice of "Hsiang-t'u" literature. The main theme of his poems, his attempt to delineate the reality of a Chinese people in Taiwan, has resulted in writing with a plain, straight-forward diction like that once employed by mainland poets of the 1940s. He has recently become the head of the Department of Fine Arts at Tunghai University in Taichung.

Poetry:

Young China, 1980
Mother, 1982

The Song of Greece

Dedicated to the youths demonstrating before
the Athens National Museum on April 3, 1975.

"Let us hold our hands tight,
And the world will promise us sunlight. . . ."[1]
This is the song the Greeks sing.

But look!
The falling altar of Apollo
Rumbles down from the Olympus peak
To the deep bottom of the Aegean Sea.

How recall those days
When fauns were in their banquets;
How recall the dark fragrance
Of olive groves in bright sunlight?
Blind Homer,
Playing his harp,
Begins softly to sing:

Do you remember still the Trojan War?
One night, the western sky burned red,
The ocean waters seethed with heat,
Men howled, horses neighed,
Gods and ghosts wept.

Do you remember still
The iron hooves of Turks
Crushing our ancestors' bones?

Do you remember still
Fleets of the British Empire
Sailing into our bays?

Do you remember still
Clamoring Nazi tanks
Among our dry fields?

Do you remember still
The Citibank
Overlooking our presidential palace?[2]

Oh! Greece!
Here, a weeping, marching group
In the streets of Athens.
Here, an angry, marching group
In the streets of Athens.
Here, a dying, marching group
In the streets of Athens.

I want once more to hear,
What were you singing?
"Democracy!"
I want once more to hear,
What were you shouting?

'Democracy!"
I want once more to hear,
What were you wanting?
"Democracy!"
I want to hear once more,
For what did you strive?
"Democracy!"

Author's notes:

[1] This is a song taught me by a Greek friend, Galatis.

[2] My friend Xaris said, "This is our presidential palace. Across from it is Citibank. This square is called Constitution Square. The Americans called it Citibank Square."

Chinatown

—New York, November 1976

Here, people buy
Beancakes, leeks;
They eat Cantonese deep-fried yams,
Shanghai rice dumplings,
Szechwan chili-diced chicken,
And roast Peking duck.

Here, someone wearing short gowns of thin gauze,
After walking out of the elevator
On the fifteenth floor,
Kneels at the buddhist chapel, prays.
On the wall, a red posted paper reads:
"Because of poor ventilation,
Please burn only one incense stick."

Someone passes the fruit stands,
Cries out, "Oh! Look!
Persimmons!"

Anxiously, someone reads different versions of Chinese newspapers,
Someone rehearses "Yang Kuei-fei Getting Drunk,"
In a high-pitched voice, singing,
"If you obey and listen
To my wish. . . ."
Someone listens to his old father:
"Study well,
What has the Fishing Island to do with you?"

Walking home after finishing work at a restaurant, someone
Passes through the empty streets
(The fifteenth moon of the month is round and round)
Passes a heap of stinking wastes,
Passes underneath buildings clattering of mahjong, and

Suddenly hears the singing:
"Plum flowers, plum flowers,
Are all over,
The more bitter
the coldness, the more blossoms;
The steadfast plum flowers
Are symbols of our great China!"

"Look at the plum flowers
Blooming everywhere,
Once there is land,
There is the flower,
It fears neither wind nor snow,
Nor ice nor frost,
It is our national flower!"

The young student
Leans against the wall,
Starts to cry.

Climbing the Mountain

On the signboard:
"4.4 miles to Gauze Cap Mt."
Signed, The Mountain Climbers Association.

Among the newly build apartment buildings
It still a small piece of farmland.
It's December, now,
Only empty rice stalks and heaps of hay remain,
And a few white-feathered chickens, pecking for food.

Someone paved the road, good square slabs;
Land rising gradually to both sides
Is terraced into ladder-paddies,

Planted with rice, sugar-cane, vegetables;
Very often, around this corner
Is a plantation of sweet potatoes;
Also papaya trees, and large yam leaves in the fields.

A bespectacled student walking in the front
Loudly asks,
"Old man,
When did you plant this sugar-cane?"
The man in the field raises his head,
Chuckling.

Ascending, we see
The flat land on both banks of the Tamsui River,
And the ugly buildings densely grouped.
Further,
Within view are the mountain ranges around Taipei,
Magnificent still;
Further,
We see the big river,
And the golden rippling sea,
And watery paddies
Reflecting a blue sky.

Ascending further,
Taipei has become very small.
There are songstresses singing
Managers representing U.S. and Japanese investments,
Poets writing poetry,
Assemblymen assembling,
Professors professing,
And painters . . .
Further,
Taipei is such a tiny spot,
Motorcycles, only, and taxis whizzing down the streets,
Prostitutes standing on corners,
Young drunken people crying in bars,
Nihilists become desperate, mad. . . .

When a group of dogs barked,
A man with a lantern came from the darkness
Asking,
"Where are you going?"

"Downhill."

Elegy to Li Shuang-tse

Why did you have to die?
Why do you not live
To take a look tonight? Taipei:

Watch the best show at the Armed Forces Arts Center,
Hsu Lu and Kuo Hsiao-chuang
Sing their operatic "An Awakened Dream in the Garden."
Also, the black limousine,
Arrives, seven-thirty, and
An old man, half-paralyzed,
Steps down with his nurse,
Walks shakily on red carpets;
People to both sides of the passage stand,
Respectfully call, "Ambassador!"

Or watch, at half-time,
Elegant front-row women
Argue whether the first play in which Mei Lang-fang
Acted after the 1945 recovery of Nanking
Was "Kue-fei Getting Drunk" or "Hsiang Yu Bidding Farewell."

Or listen, the chattering,
The exchange concerning diabetes, hypertension,
Pulmonary emphysema, atherosclerosis.

Why did you have to die?
Why do you not live
To take a look late at night? Taipei:

The woman in a high coiffure
Who sits beside a piano
Sips with smiles her martini.

And artists, and poets
Wearing bright shirts of color,
Signing French chansons.

To see the waiter pouring wine
    for an old American man;
Who, when he touches the waiter's buttocks,
Receives a provocative smile.
Wine Cave, the Ambassador Hotel,
Where you can stay drunk 'til two in the morning.

Why did you have to die?
Why do you not live
To take a look? prosperous Taipei:

Hsin-Lin Restaurant,
In Jen Ai Road, 4th Section,
A fashion designer, returned from New York,
Christian Dior scarf around the neck,
Twists his moustache with his fingers.

In Rokujo-dori, in Chung Shan North Road,
Porridge and rice wine served,
Merchants embrace female entertainers,
Loudly sing, "Sakura, Sakura."

Please, look!
Prosperous Taipei:
The new variety show by Ts'ui T'ai-ch'ing,
And Liu Wen-cheng, powder on his face,
Sing, "Plum flowers, plum flowers,"
Pai Chia-li finally marries an Indonesian millionaire.

Young people in the streets,
In and out of cinemas,
Wear T-shirts, "University of Washington,"
Eat T-bone steaks,
Chew gum,
Chat about Ch'in Hsiang-lin, murders, mahjong,
And Canada's newly enacted immigrant laws.

Oh! Shuang-tse,
Why did you have to die?
Why do you not live?

Let the gale disperse our tears,
The tides abrade our sorrows;
Let us once more see clearly
The place we dearly love:

The red sun rises from Tamsui, where you lived;
Fishing boats return from the ocean,
People rush about in the harbor,
Hauling fish, nets, logs.
The moving ferry boats
Transport merchants, students, old and young;
Workers at Kuan-yin Mountain
Haul with hemp strings stone slabs, rocks.

Large rice paddies,
Fluttering green foliage;
Old farmers wandering in fields,
Bending, occasionally examining
Solid ears of corn;
Tilling and digging, they're nothing.

New high-rises,
Workers, scaling empty structures,
Carry sand and limestone on their backs;
Thick in sweat from their foreheads
They walk, firm in step;
One miss, their bones are crushed.

People sitting in shop, drinking soy-bean milk,
When the village secretary enters, hello,
The mid-month moon is bright,
Shining on the open ground of the regional office;
Everybody claps,
"Let's sing 'Mending the Net' once more."

Shuang-tse, oh! Shuang-tse,
Look. The elementary boys fall in,
So evenly paying tribute to their flag;
The song in which you once asked,
"Who plants the rice?" Who catches the fish?"
Who makes the clothes?"[1]
They will remember.

Look at this young teacher;
On the blackboard, he draws a begonia leaf:
"This is the Great Wall, this the T'ai-heng Mountain,
The Yellow and Yangtze Rivers are forever running."
We look again,
And also see the high Mount Tai-Tun and meandering Tamsui,
And water buffaloes, rice orchids.[2]

Oh! Shuang-tse,
Do you know
Wu Chu-liu died, but
Old Yang Kuei continued gardening at Tunghai University?
This old drummer still beats,
Advocates "Freedom and Equality."[3]

See, young people who once became drunk and cried,
They have wiped their tears,
No bafflement, no lingering;
They now leave for the high hills and big rivers,
To the mines, fishing villages,
Factories and fields.

Dear Shuang-tse,
Can you still see,

Can you still now see
The old camp-ground you once irrigated and dug?
It now blossoms on an entire hill of flowers.

Translator's note: Li Shuang-tse was a young artist who advocated writing and singing new songs with local color. He drowned while trying to save some students in a river.

Note numbers 1,2, and 3 indicate phrases taken from Li's songs.

Shih Shan-chi (1945–   )

Although Shih was once a modernist, as reflected in the collection entitled *The Umbrella Season,* his poetic style changed drastically after the controversy over "*Hsiang-tu* literature" in the 1970s. He began to use a much plainer diction to focus on the narration of social events, events often related to the tragic history of the Chinese people. Like Chiang Hsun, however, Shih's poetic practice falls into the trap of a kind of narration in which, instead of artistically altering his subject matter, he just records or reports events.

Poetry:

The Umbrella Season, 1969.
Poems of Shih Shan-chi, 1981.

Fording

—For the teachers drowned when fording

Teachers, really
Was that time the last time;
In a memory of numerous fordings,
Was that day the last day?

Breakfast done,
A goodbye wave for families,
And the usual trek to Hualien Creek, freely
Facing the only "way" to Shan-hsing Elementary.
There was no other exit,
No other way.
No way. No exit.
You lifted your dresses, gave your selfless love,
To dispense, among all small friends
Who need love, care, initiation, teaching;
Teachers, you exhausted your selfless love
To test, to interrupt gushing torrents
In mid-autumn, in an overflowing creek
You went, your selfless love, small as a scoop of water,
To emerge in a great sea, to fill it with boundless love.
Teachers, your patient instruction
Brought examples, analyses, illustrations;
These girls learned
Human dignity, chastity, the steadfast guardianship
Of native Eastern Taiwan,
With labor, hardship;
Like the pioneers, the guards from past to present,
These now guard the future;
They farm the land, endlessly till soil
To banish barrenness;
They raise pigs, grow vegetables, pick fruit, plant flowers,
And refuse to drift outside,
Refuse to degenerate, outside;
Where their bodies, well sustained by their parents,
Could easily plunge to worldliness,
They refuse that fall, that dispersion
To dark corners of the black market,
Where sex-transactions and V.D. grow;
They refuse the fiery plunge into organized prostitution
Feeding the underground lust, money,
Leaving victims in fiery pits,
Burning in unquenchable flames

Feebly crying for help,
Rising, falling in the city's clamor,
In hopelessness' dark heart;
Whose plan could rescue them?
Teachers, you advised always
Not to be bound, to be trampled by outsiders,
Not to use the flesh as barter for cheap living,
Or for cheap money to sustain poor families.
Poor, we may be, but we stand
Proudly in our native land.
We raise pigs, plant vegetables, pick fruit, grow flowers,
Cultivate, with blood and sweat, and till our soil;
Our work means the national dictum:
"To establish the order of the universe,
To establish the lives of the common people."
We will not mar our matrix,
The matrix of our nation
From which we multiply, continue.
When someone fondles, tramples our nation's matrix,
Might our race not survive in such imminence?

Teachers, those boys
Jump and laugh.
With patience, once, you followed them,
Played, laughed like big sisters
On the hills, you taught them plants' names;
In the plantations, you taught sowing,
In the orchards, weeding,
At the seashore, fishing;
In narrow-terraced rice paddies.
You instructed how to dig the ditches, to irrigate,
To listen for the ripening of corn.
Against the coming typhoons,
You taught them how to repair roofs and fences,
To cage chickens and ducks,
To examine cow-pens, pig-pens;
You warned them against wandering outside,

Or letting fields and gardens go barren;
Against entanglement with outside problems,
And following the bad examples of those outside;
You told them not to stand on city streets and lanes,
As pimps, shamelessly grabbing,
Not to watch over massage-parlor doors,
Not to gamble in pinball-machine shops,
Not to be gambling-house bodyguards;
Not to be drug addicts, rapists, burglars.

Teachers, you taught them not to wander;
To guard their native land, Eastern Taiwan;
Taught them to marry, to raise families.
They use their thick shoulders,
They graze, till, chop, and lift,
And use their wide chest to embrace the great earth;
They sing from deep in their bosoms
Graceful songs of the Aborigines.
In a vast plain, they circle about,
Hand in hand, shoulder to shoulder
To dance to the year of the harvest.
They pray the industrious sun will punctually rise
To shine on the hard-working people, on the cattle.
The papayas are ripe, the watermelons sweet;
The people graze cattle, till lands, chop wood, and lift things;
This, the teachers taught, the same as
    "To establish the order of the universe,
    To establish the lives of the common people."
Don't let outsiders exploit, oppress, and threaten;
Don't let outsiders trample, suck, and chew on us.

Teachers, really was
That time the last time;
With your casual farewell to your families,
Really was
That day the last day?
You left no wills, but

You left the other side of the bank,
You left your young friends
To stand on the playground,
Or sit in the classrooms,
Waiting for love, care, guidance.
Who would believe
That morning was the last morning.
Please do not worry;
Though you've left,
The world remains ours,
A positive, progressive world
Where all, from all walks of life, work.

Teachers, there is now a bridge
Between the banks of the creek,
A bridge of love you constructed,
Selfless, wide, long.
Walking over it,
People feel the strength you left in the concrete;
Your selfless love supports every inch, and
People crossing the bridge remember your tragic fording—
On a mid-autumn morning,
In the overwhelming water,
You lifted your clothes, fording,
And filled the universe with selfless love.

Chan Ch'e (1954–   )

Often dealing with country themes, Chan Ch'e's poems represent a genuine return to the rural; in them he capably uses simple images to express the sorrow and helplessness of "the little people" in society's great, turning wheel. Although his poems dramatically describe social events, he never sacrifices the artistic integrity of his imagery, and consciously strives for a well developed poetic structure. In addition to his other poetry, he writes poems for children.

Poetry:

Earth, Please Speak Up, 1983
The History of Hands, 1986

The Mirror

A tree by the river
Looked at its old shape;
As evening bent over the foot of the hill,
My mother bent at the riverside;
Not knowing what a mirror
Or what a beautiful wife was;
She only washed, and washed
Dirty clothes from the rice fields.

Father, at that time, was fighting far away;
Like a floating cloud in exodus
He flew up and down the skies
    between the Taiwan Strait and the Indian Ocean,
Between the Chinese Republic and Japanese Imperialists.

At that time
The sun was a mirror without reflection;
China was the world's mirror,
And Taiwan the dust wiped from it.

Now, everywhere is a mirror;
Is it civilization
Or enlightenment?
I look at the mirror
But not seeing myself,
Let me just write my lyrics then.

Frying Fish

When the rice paddies slowly dry, and
The sky's clouds slowly begin to crack,
My father's wrinkles grow deeper,
Oh! Such a map is his face,
Like the cracked bottom of a pot;
Fighting and bloodshed,
Intertwining, unrecognizable traces;
This is our green home,
Our history of the yellow race.

Every time father watches mother
Frying fish,
The process seems to him like
Battleships, bones, corpses;

The fish is done
Like a roasted sweet potato,
Browned without blood
But done through pain.

A Broken Bowl

At the end of the Second World War,
Upon Japan's surrender,
All the soldiers in Southeast Asia
Began looking back
To the Strait of Taiwan.

Bringing only a broken bowl,
Grandfather begged from people all the way
On his return to Taiwan.
The broken bowl
Is his only memory.

On the evening of the August Seventh Flood,
When water rushed to the rice fields, and
In the morning, the farmers' feet
Where all above ground,
All the villagers in Central Taiwan
Turned their heads eastward,
And looked toward the central mountain ranges.

Father brought only this broken bowl,
Begging the entire way
So I could survive.
When we finally moved to Eastern Taiwan,
The broken bowl
Became his only memory.
When cannons sound off on the television screen,

Grandfather's long white eyebrows droop in worry:
What shall we do? What shall we do?
Why is there again fighting in Southeast Asia?
Why is there again fighting in Southeast Asia?

She Is Not Mute

1.

Many fingers point,
Quietly, she could care less,
And follows men into a tiny room, casually,
Quietly.
Without distinction of classes,
A man wants her, she must stand;
A man slaps her,
She is quiet,
A man spits at her,
She is quiet;
But, definitely, she is not mute.
Other prostitutes, friends,
Declare prices by the door;
She sits, keeps quiet,
But she is not mute.

Like a lost grey pidgeon,
Like a bundle of Chinese cabbage just pulled from the ground,
She is quiet,
But she is not mute.
She always stands by the riverside,
Flowing water reflects moonlight,
Flows away time,
Brings her childhood years—
"My mother was a mute."

2.

She says,
"When I was a baby,
Mother used to put me by the side of the field.
She was busy picking rice ears,
Digging sweet potatoes,
Also, picking peanuts and corn left in the field."
She says,
"When I was three,
One day, mother forgot me in a faraway place;
She busily rushed home at night,
And arriving with her bag of sweet potatoes
Remembered leaving me beneath a tree;
Father chided, scolded, beat her;
Quietly, she rushed back,
And I returned to the hill once again;
In the small, thatched hut,
Under the dim, yellow candle light,
I stared with my big, black eyes."
She says,
"When I was thirteen,
And learned how to sow, irrigate, weed, and fertilize,
I also knew how to reap, thresh, and bag,
How to chop down sugar cane,
And embroider the most beautiful design of an apron.
One day,
I became attracted to the boy down hill."
She says,
"One day
A stout man came,
And gave mother a sum of money;
I was afraid, but yielded,
And obediently followed the man away;
Not a tear I shed,
But only gave a quick glimpse down hill,
Where there was smoke in the chimney of the boy's house;
Hurriedly, I left . . ."

She says,
"Mother didn't say a word,
Couldn't utter a word;
Tears hung in her dry, dark face,
Her dry, thick lips moved,
Her dry, thin finger trembled, but
She could utter not a single sound.
Mother was mute."
She says,
"When I first started making that sort of money,
Mother came once to see me;
She came into my lane,
Entered the small house where I lived;
In the dim light
We couldn't see each other's face,
But vaguely I saw—
Tears hung in her dry, dark face,
Her dry, thick lips moved,
Her dry, thin finger trembled;
She said, in signs,
'I . . . was wrong.' "
She says,
"Mother used quick, remorseful signs, to say
'Forgive me, it's because of your younger brother and sister,
They have to go to school;
Forgive your father, who now is dead;
On the hill, all the land deeds,
Sweet potatoes, peanuts, corn are sold,
But we do not have enough money to ransom you.'
Mother used confused signs, saying
'Forgive me, forgive me . . .' she cried."

        3.

She is not mute,
She says, "My name is White Cloud,

All men have called me White Cloud."
She must have been, really,
A clean and pure white cloud.
White Cloud has adopted a small girl;
Every afternoon,
She must leave the girl in someone's house;
She does not know why;
Why she must forget her name,
Her ancestors, blood-ties,
And let men call her "White Cloud,"
Why she has to leave home
To drift in east Taiwan, Hualien, Yilan,
Taipei, T'aoyuan, and finally in this
Tiny Ku Ling-lin.

I see from White Cloud,
And from the eyes of her little daughter,
Kindness like an aurora,
And sweet, pure mother love.

White Cloud is not a mute;
Since the Manchus, Dutch, Spanish, and Japanese
Have occupied Taiwan,
Her parents, ancestors, relatives, clan people
Were not mute;
She definitely is not mute.
She was originally an aborigine, who liked to sing,
Like the mountain wind blowing into the canyon,
Like the ocean breeze coming into the canyon,
She was originally an aborigine, who liked to sing;
Her ancestors were the proud and dignified
Song-loving tribesmen;
But like an ancient timber sawed apart,
Or a fierce bear trapped,
Their pride eventually was defeated.
Like earthworms falling into water,
Or crickets hidden in the soil,
Their songs were choked off.

Like an uphill trail trampled by a generation of people,
She waits to be trampled,
But she definitely is not mute.
The tip of her tongue is wild grass leaves,
Clear river pebbles are her teeth;
When she sings aloud,
Gusts blow over leaves of grass,
Storms beat on the pebbles and rocks;
For generations,
An uphill trail to be trampled by people,
And the land bearing all historical crimes
Will witness the everlasting, unrighteous mountain.
When her clan people, ancestors, parents,
When her soul and her little daughter's
Talk and sing loudly once again.

Old Liu's Dawn

The Dawn's Ceremony

1.

In order to wake the living, who sleep,
Earth already has begun
The most solemn ceremony.

Dawn stretches its back,
Stands up. . . .

Awaking are the forests,
The birds and insects,
The brooks and rivers,
The mountain's outlines
And the eaves of farm houses.

In a dead, silent cemetary,
The green grass on the graves awakens;
Even the corner of the gravestone tablet
Brightly grins with dawn's arrival.

2.

Amidst the wood in the mountain,
The field battle troops
March at the blowing bugle,
Loud, clear, sharp,
Spreading wide, far, away;
The sound seems to match the last crow of the cock.

Soldiers, one after another,
Like green spots,
Emerge from the dark wood;
Right along the narrow oxcart lane
They walk down from the terraced rice fields in flickering dawn.

Every green spot bears a yellowish backpack,
Every backpact sports the slanting sprout of a gun barrel.
Like a dot connecting to another dot,
No words or sentences,
No conversation. . . .

3.

Quietly, over the cool, snowy horizon,
The sun spews out golden red powders.
Before day's arrival,
This is the most solemn ceremony;
The ceremony of dawn
Is coming to its end—

Following closely
Is the race more difficult than any other;
People who are awakened by dawn
Will use their lives to make the long journey—

The race of livelihood and survival.
There is no starting gun,
No cheerleaders,
No formal running lanes with white lines.

He Starts Before Dawn

1.

Before nature holds its dawn ceremony,
Before the awakening of lives who enter the race,
He, Old Liu,
Is awake.
No alarm clock,
But automatically, with precision,
He wakes before dawn.

Most lives quicken with the dawn,
But Old Liu wakes dawn
To deliver with his hands the world's news
Before dawn awakens.

Old liu
Has the duty of newscarrier;
One year,
Two, three, four years,
The Old Liu who carries on the newscarrier duty,
Who came to Taiwan from the mainland,
Who once was an army officer,
He wants to start before dawn.

Before dawn,
Old Liu begins the race more difficult than any other;
He uses the second half of his luckily remaining life
To journey on the never completed running lane of time, and
In the arena of livelihood and survival;
Old Liu wants to start before dawn,

Like a predawn attack in the Sino-Japanese War.
Target—
Big streets, small lanes of towns and cities,
Half-opened iron gates;
Well lined apartment building windows
Are like peepholes of a watch tower.

2.

Old Liu gets out of bed,
Turns on the light at the bedside;
Light falls on his bumpy face
Crisscrossed with wrinkles,
Like a Chinese face in modern history,
Old, but steadfast.

Old Liu swiftly dons a white blouse,
And khaki shorts, plus a green towel;
Simple, light, convenient,
This is his new uniform.

Then, he pulls out his job tool:
A sturdy, heavy-duty bicycle,
Or the horse he uses
To make his living in the battlefield of life.

Old Liu mounts his old horse,
Skillfully holds to the handles,
Faces the morning breeze,
And rides fast.

3.

By the newspaper distributor's door
He loads his newspaper bag full,
And prepares life's ambushes.

Riding his old horse,
Right foot on the pedal,

Left still holding onto the ground,
He strikes a match and lights a cigarette.

Throwing away the cigarette butt,
He inhales deeply the early morning air, and
Turns on the horse;
His body leaning to the front,
His right foot pushing hard,
He rushes in to the labyrinth of lanes
And complex households.

Street at Dawn

1.

Dawn rushes to recover territory taken by darkness,
Old Liu rushes himself,
And passes with the dawn through every street and lane in town.

When he goes in and out of the
Complex and regulated streets,
Dawn sends the signal;
Stripes of gold,
Start stretching

Like fingers bringing in the gifts of life,
Golden stripes enter every lane and street,
Enter every half-opened window.
They want to sweep open slumbering eyes,
To tell the living sleepers
—Dawn is here.

It is dawn
That follows behind his back,
Then overtakes him in the front.
Old Liu's shadow creeps forward
Now to be stretched by the light of dawn.

Whenever he brakes
To throw a newspaper into a sleepy courtyard,
Old Liu's stretched shadow is shortened by the rising dawn.

2.

Watching every dark blue house number plate
Glisten in the dawn,
Old Liu skillfully, precisely delivers his papers;
By the time he turns the corner to "Shantung Snack Bar,"
The singing garbage-collecting truck
Is coming to the end of the lane.

The tune of "Maiden's Prayer"
Freshens and warms;
The truck passes through the streets,
Refreshing and flat.

Slow and relaxing is the tempo of the "Maiden's Prayer,"
But garbage collectors are swift and busy.

As is holding tight to the meaning of life,
The bean-milk store by the street side
Bubbles with spreading white mists.
On the bamboo steamers
Are shiny, white little meat buns,
Reflecting in the aurora of dawn.
In the large steaming containers
Are the large meat buns,
Healthy and succulent;
The soft and fragrant smell
Has spread to the streets,
Attracting hungry people.

In the streets,
Early wakers
Have come out;
Those who are awake and half awake

Have heard or smelled the day's beginning,
And the wide, spreading turmoil delivered with dawn.

3.

Old Liu just came out from the bean-milk shop,
And encounters a group of elementary school children who,
Like small ducks with heavy wings on their backs,
Walk in unsteady strides;
They say hello to Old Liu like he's an old acquaintance,
And leisurely walk on the modern, wide flat road paved by for-
    mer generations.

"It would have been nice if I had gone to school. . ."
"It would have been nice if my wife and children were here. . ."
Old Liu
Finally quits thinking of his past;
Only one street remains;
His body leaning forward,
His right foot pushing heavily on the pedal,
He and his tired horse
Swiftly glide into the last street,
Starting with "number one" in "lane one". . .

Now he comes to the street corner
Once pasted with posters and flyers;
Still, remnants of paper are stuck by the corner wall.
Last winter, this street corner,
And the telephone poles along the street,
All were pasted with election papers and brochures.
Old Liu was true to his life;
He could not finish counting how many posters there were;
Like every citizen
He was concerned about this election
Symbolizing "democracy" and "justice."

"If I had taken that man's bribe. . ."
"If I had insisted on not casting the vote. . ."

Old Liu finally stops recollecting.
Paper remnants by the corner wall
Grow with moss in the morning dew;
Somewhat like his bumpy face
Deep with tracks of wrinkles;
His face looks old and sturdy,
Like the fate of Chinese in modern history.
Like the fate of modern Chinese
Passing on a journey of ups and downs,
Having been tested by history,
And simultaneously pushing history onward.
Old Liu has delivered his last newspaper.

4.

Old Liu saved himself a newspaper;
He wants carefully to analyze
The news from the other side of the strait.
All these years
He has delivered and read newspapers,
He has been capable of finishing reading
This forever three-paged newspaper.

The crowded Chinese characters in the paper,
Once like dense wild geese landing
On the wide, snowy plain of the North,
Appeared to Old Liu like a dark pine woods before him;
Now, they are like ants which recognize him, and
Move the modern knowledge into his eyes;
True knowledge which enriches him
Like sweet honey, well stored in his mind.

His eyesight fails,
But knowledge makes him young;
His job is base,
But his life is healthy.
Old Liu is no longer the "tool" of newspaper delivery;
He is the nanny of newspapers,

The postman of newspapers, without uniform, an old soldier
Who delivers for dawn's eyes the true and false news to the world.

Exhausted, he rides his bike back,
Facing the bright, rising morning sun,
And climbs a slope;
Relaxing, he breathes on the slope of dawn,
Today, oh, today's dawn
Is also the dawn of tomorrow!

Author's note: from the literary supplement of the *China Times* and also from *Chung-hua Monthly*, I have been introduced to Ai Ch'ing. His poetry moves people deeply, and I cannot forget the description of the Chinese village, layer after layer, in his poems. I have further realized the poet's fear in an age of turmoil. The "dawn" image of his poems resurrected the poetic seed of "Old Liu" in my imagination. Inevitably, or quite willingly, therefore, the language of this poem is partially under his influence.

Yang Tse (1954–   )

Yang studied philosophy and English literature at National Tai-wan University, and is now doing graduate work at Princeton University. A contemporary of Lo Chih-ch'eng, Yang shares the same romantic ideals and philosophical interpretation of life. Yang Mu, in a preface for Yang Tse's book of poetry, pointed out that the major themes in his poems are love and poetry. In love there is sympathy, and with poetry Yang Tse derives from life its vital forces, conquering death.

Poetry:

The Birth of the Rose School, 1977
Somewhat in the Fatherly Kingdom, 1980

Somewhat in the Kingdom of His Majesty, No. 2

Heavy Snow.
On the nineteenth of the month.

It's only a lonely, impatient, evening downpour,
Rushing from a deserted past.
Looking out from a window,
Through the withering lotus

Like wandering ghosts at midnight,
In large drops of rain,
I vaguely see
The lonely shadow of that person
Fleeing,

He removes his straw raincoat,
Leaves the snowy straw hat on the table.
(I can feel his stormy days are behind his back)
He says
"*Tempus fugit,*
Have you all forgotten gradually
The legend of the river snow?
Forgotten the regrets of fishing alone
All these years. . ."

"*Tempus fugit,*
But the ancient river snow remains unmelted,
You should remember the day of the river-crossing;
How many old friends had turned into scattered corpses?
Their blood ran through rivers and valleys,
Their flesh and bone commingled.
Who shall I ask for the remains of Our Majesty
And his glorious past?
Rainy snowflakes, rainy snowflakes,
How did he expand this country's territory?
In the vast river snow,
His Majesty's kingdom has ever since sunk. . ."

Putting his hand behind his back,
He paces the room.
His steps are heavy with a weight I don't know,
Vaguely, the soughing winter storm has turned into
The low chants of entrapped fish:
"The kingdom of His Majesty
And old friends of the past
Are a shattered reality of a real fantasy
In a world of hooks and lures.

We have had life mutations,
And were taught and quietly guided
By requited love, and births. . ."

"Oh! The ancient snow remains unmelted,
His Majesty's kingdom remains unrecovered.
How shall I pass on to you my own unfulfilled ambition:
To liberate myself from fishing alone. . ."
All this time, he turns his back to me.
Like a high-pitched historical narration, outside the window
Events break into a lonely, impatient, evening downpour.
In an unreachable countryland,
Heavy snow continues to fall. . . .

Lo Chih-ch'eng (1955–   )

After graduating from the Philosophy Department at National Taiwan University, Lo went in 1981 to study at the University of Wisconsin. His poetry has a flavor of philosophical lyricism. Although he emphasizes an intuitive apprehension of reality, his poetic ambiguity is not characterized by surrealistic playfulness; rather, it reflects his convictions about an ontological view of life. He stresses that poetry is not the ultimate goal, because poetry is only part of life and human existence. We find in Lo's poetry a force of life that is incessantly evolving and manifesting itself.

Poetry:

Painting Albums, 1975
The Book of Light, 1979
The Book of Obliquity, 1981

A Candle Has Slept In Its Own Flame

A candle has slept in its own flame now.

Baby, let us gently walk down the stairs,
And clean up the messy world before you go to bed.
The little tantrum you had on the carpet
We will bring into your warm blanket to melt.

A candle has slept in its own flame now.
The cradle of time softly rocks.
Death lightly breathes,
Baby, let us pass it by
Holding on to our secret mission, looking to eternity for help.

Let us fly a kite on the beach!
From the cleft of the night curtain ripped open by meteors,
Let us find out the schedule of the stars.
Let us ski on your hair,
But refrain from disturbing our civilization.
A candle has slept, like a wonderful brush,
Wielding deliriously to the sky.
Let us go to the bakery before it is closed,
And purchase tomorrow's breakfast.
If, later on, you prefer,
We will pilfer the navigation map of the globe.

A candle has slept in its own flame now.
Blow it out with your graceful mouth, baby.
Death in us grows bigger and bigger;
I wonder, what would it feel between our love?
Baby, you are so exhausted, yet so pretty,
And you have spread out on the dresser your attachments
Before you sleep.

Hsiang Yang (1955–   )

At the end of the 1970s, after modern poetry in Taiwan was caught in the pendulous swing from Western to Chinese models, there was still no definite clue to its direction. The emergence of the Sunlight Ensemble Poetry Society, comprised of promising young poets, however, indicated the dedication and unyielding spirit of these young poets. Hsiang Yang, a major figure in the group, represents a new prospect among these young poets, a confirmation of both modernism and realism in contemporary Chinese poetry. Hsiang and his colleagues write profusely, as if trying to replace with their works the empty slogans and moanings of senior poets.

Hsiang has a good control of modernist and realist diction, yet commits himself to neither. He is one of the few young poets to experiment profusely with local Taiwanese dialects in poetry. While he conveys a strong concern for social reality, he loves art for its pure aesthetic value. He once compared himself to a gingko tree, which uses a siphon (love) to draw water from the soil and strengthen the inner xylum (tradition). The tree's sieving tubes (wisdom) are used to distill nutrients from the air, expanding and exploring the elasticity of the outer phloem (modernity).

Hsiang graduated as a Japanese major from Chinese Cultural University, and is now chief editor of the literary supplement to the *Chih-li Evening News*.

Poetry:

Anticipation of the Gingko Tree, 1977
Seeds, 1980
Ten-line Poems, 1984

Time and Tide, 1985
Songs of the Earth, 1985
My Cares (English Translations), 1985

Sailing in the Rain

In the thick rain, the ink-splash rain,
In the solitary raising of hands,
The expectant eyes,
Let me take you sailing
Down a dream, and dreamlike rivers.
Gently, gently we glide
Into the winds and tides of five thousand years,
To the rocky shore where
Dignity has confronted willful pride these five thousand years,
Toward the somber firmament of rain,
Toward the vast universe of sea,
Toward the tears of begonia blood,
The grid of scorching veins.[1]

Hard we sail! In the rain
From which night and dawn refuse to separate,
I hold my pen for a lamp,
And call a dawn in blackest night,
To make the morning rooster rouse
Silent China! That China may grow to grandeur!
On every inch of blood-drenched earth,
Plow peaceful acres,
Through every clod of tear-drenched soil,
Lay tear-free furrows;
Step by step, track down joy
Through the face of darkness and sorrow.

And in these hundred years, our fathers
Never once dreamed
They were waking lions, or dragons
Dancing in the clouds!
A century of battle-fires,
Of uncleansed bloodstains,
A century of war-ashes
Still lie above irreparable ruins;
A century of foreign might
Compacted, chewed, devoured us.
The one thing China has not known is light.
The fields were not tilled, but shrapnel fell to plow them;
The trees were not yet fully grown, but they fashioned guns.

The impact our fathers sustained
We can but surmise in silence,
Reading our textbooks,
And chewing on the aftermath of the Opium War.
In this thick rain, drop upon drop.
Falls the inexorable sorrow of modern China,
From the hands reaching for help
In the billows of the South China Sea,
To the footprints running for refuge
On the borders of Laos and Vietnam;
From the upheavals and calamities of the old country,
to the homeless driftings abroad,
The bitter struggle of the diaspora.
In our papers, wherever we turn,
the pages brim with China,
Sailing lonely in the rain.

In the rain, we too are sailing,
Repelling demons and the roses of vanity,
Roar of applause, spittle of curses.
We are neither lion dormant,
Nor dragon from distant Cathay,
Just Chinese,
And the Chinese soil is beneath our feet,

In our blood and tears.
Warmly we tread the breadth of
The begonia leaf.
No need of dreams, we can take to our hearts
The winds and tides of five thousand years,
The myriad miles of home.

Sweep away the mists of gloom.
Let us grow!
In a wild and stormy night.
Though leaves may fall,
More fruits will swell.
Leaping from our dream,
Let us take a walk on the rocky shore
Of dignity and willful pride,
Let us watch the vast universe of sea.
Soon, the bright day will dawn,
But till then, in the thick rain, the ink-splash rain,
In the bold raising of hands,
And the determined eyes,
Let me take you sailing.

1. Translator's note: the map of China is often likened to a begonia leaf.

Ten Lines: Autumn

Unable to hold on to the dry branches,
Leaves tumble to the morning-chilled pond.
A man with an umbrella walks past the dewy lake,
Listens to a pine cone drop from the right of the woods,
Calls out in surprise:

"Is this the way you come?"
Ripples and echoes linger on the hallow surface of water,
Duckweed stands aside, leaving the clear mountain reflections
To kiss the sky, blue after rain.
This is deep, deep autumn now.

Ten Lines: On Seed

Unless I depart resolved from my dependent coronet,
I will only bend and hear the wilting sound of the twigs.
All fragrances, butterflies, and yeterdays
Eventually will disperse with the wind.
Unless I reject the green foliage's protection,
I can prepare to receive the shocks of the breaking soil.

Choosing to dwell in the mountain,
I would miss the space of the wild plain.
Living by the seashore
I would not be cleansed by running brooks.
Since there is no absolute, I drift, I wander,
Seeking only a steady fitting land To settle, to multiply.

Floral Invasions

"Distant fragrance invades the ancient road,
Morning greenness connects the barren city."

—Po Ch'u-i

Now Gen'ral. I am the nightwatch frontier guard, come
From the moat, drunk, singing, singing, come
T' report, well, to preport, shir, that it is fair spring. And,

Shir, well, the news 'f flowers, that news
Is right this minute invadin' our fair, fair shitty.
Ya hear them drums? Them Gongs?

Mpum, mpum
Clang . . . Clang
Mpum. . .

Now Gen'ral, Shir, No time t' rest. Enemy commander's name's
Spring. 'S fair spring, I think. 'N his unit's called
Flower news. Please, shir, you just shend the order. The order
That all units shtand. Ready, that is. Jush shend the order
Down. Frontier guard'll messag—missage—Frontier guard'll
Take it, shir. Please, gen'ral, deliver your frosty old
Dignity—'scuse me—send down your blood-and-tear geography
   map.
Hear that wind moaning? Think of it this way, shir.
All them senior citizens, east of the River, and
All them three-thousand soldiers, them young soldiers of yours,
Is ready. Waitin', shir, for this here moment of decision.
Mpum, Mpum
Clang. . .

Gen'ral, shir, I . . . I'm the mess'ger. Enemy's already croshed
The moat. City gate's already done in. This here Fair Spring,
Shir, and Spring News, They are already . . . right this minute
   . . .
Past the guards of our citadel.

Soil and Flower

—Thoughts on poetry and language

In bright sunlight and gentle breeze,
The flower fully grows, vigorously blooms

Its face;
Provocative and charming, it
Looks to the sky,
Then looks down to the soil below;
She shows off her persistent aesthetics,
In a warm climate,
Proclaims to the wilderness:
The so-called symbolism
In her bodies, petals, stamen,
The so-called purity,
Is the passageway, spotless,
Far from the soil, leading to Heaven.

The soil is silent.
Clumsily it bears the flower and her arrogance,
Remains wordless.
But, nightly, it collects in toil the rainy dew,
To supply the exorbitant flower a daytime;
And, in daytime, it toils for nutrients
To guard the gradual invading, menacing roots,
So the flower can absorb the nutrients;
There is no
Purity, no transcendence;
There is only crudity, disorder, strength.

The prettier the flower,
The baser the soil;
Glaring with exaggeration, the flower droops,
Yet, with containment, the soil richens.
When, suddenly one night, a storm comes,
Petals and stamen leave the stem,
All return to the soil of birth and death,
To learn from the start, of living in soil, in dust,
Between blooming and withering.
Seeming dead, the flower actually lives;
In giving, receiving,
The soil without expression welcomes
Another flower's birth, its clamoring.

Grampaw's Smoking Pipe

Some time ago, some time,
I'd watch grampaw's smokin' pipe.
At sunset.
Smoke'd come from the chimney, an'
From ever' paint-chipped old house there was,
There was many a strange, pretty story.

These days I hold grampaw's pipe
In the cold, in the winter I hold
The hard ole wooden crutch;
In ever' one of these clean streets,
To be picked of the rotten, stinkin' rocks and garbage.

In forty years, should I still be smokin'
Grampaw's pipe. . .
What time would that be. . .
Well, how
Would I tell my own gran'children
Their grampaw's glamorous history?

Translator's note: the original poem was written in a local Taiwanese dialect.

Liu K'o-hsiang (1957–   )

Most people know about Liu K'o-hsiang as both poet and bird-watcher. His recent publications either have dealt mostly with watching birds and their habitats, or are records of his travels to the island of Taiwan. We may say of Liu the bird-watcher that he watches with a poetic eye. On the other hand, as a poet, Liu applies the keen, scientific, bird-watcher's eye to his criticisms of human life. He belongs to a generation of young, native Taiwanese who share a deep concern not only for Taiwan's historical past, but also for the nebulous identity of Taiwan in the Chinese context. Thus, Liu's poems embrace two different approaches: a radical but realistic view of the social phenomena in Taiwan; and a lyrical escape to the world of birds, in which he forms his own microcosmic universe apart from human affairs.

Poetry:

Downstream, 1978
A Squirrel named Bambi Ts'ao, 1983
A Stray Bird's Homeland, 1984
In the Island of Slanting Heaven, 1986

A Stray Bird's Homeland

Never will I forget the days when father waited for me on the
    horizon, for me to run over to him;

The roads on which I followed him to faraway places have now
   all disappeared.
I, now middle-aged, also love to travel,
But I no longer have his shadow in front of me.

Like his students, I worry always for the future;
In the mountain hotel where he once dwelled, there is no longer
   the sound of the wooden clogs;
When the *obasan* sees me watching the view from the window,
She vaguely reminisces about him.

From the west to the east coast,
From the remote fishing village to the plateau city,
Different times, different feelings;
Exhausted, I return from drifting.
Grandmother always said we were useless intellectuals.

Here. Only here remains,
Where father once stood for a long time.
Now, I do.
In this quiet hall with incense burning,
There lies a tablet with his name on it, in the last row;
Next to him it is yet empty;
Of course, they wait for me to join them.

1970s

—For the compatriots who have drifted in Taiwan and China
for the past thirty years.

In the Ch'ing-ming festival
Rain fell on the Chiang Kai-shek Memorial Hall in Taipei;
Hundreds of thousands assembled and stood.
What days were those?
When a man with tattoos on his arm,

Cried tears in his eyes,
And a man in a Chung-shan costume, with staff in hand,
Silently watched the sky?

In the Ch'ing-ming festival,
Rain fell on the T'ien-an-Gate Square;
Half a million crowded in, rushing,
What years were those?
There was a man fluent in Japanese,
With lowered head, wordless;
There was a man raised in Tainan,
Staring far away.

Whose bronze statues
Now are erected in the city and towns in Taiwan?
Whose cremated ashes
Are sprinkled over the land of China?

Small Is Beautiful

Early in the morning,
The snipe sticks out its head from the bushes;
In a while
It silently comes to the brook's bank,
Quietly stretches out its beak,
Hunting;
Then it retraces to the bushes. . .
All winter,
Along the upper stream of Ta-tu Brook,
Snipes are all about the marshes,
Resting,
Waiting for spring.

At this time only will the north-eastern wind blow southward;
Landing from the seashore

During the ebb and flow of tides
Marsh sandpipers keep changing locations;
They cling to each other, evading the cold current,
And live a life of resting and hunting;
Little water ducklings imitate the sandpipers
Warming each other, caring for each other;
Also, grey egrets, and small white egrets. . .

Then, the ecology of the river's mouth
Forms its two banks like the strecthing arms of Buddha;
The islets are like whales floating
And rushing toward the sea;
All water fowl gradually assemble
On spacious, flat riverbeds,
In the coldest season,
One hundred of them, one thousand, then thousands. . .

Early in the morning
The blue sandpiper takes its solitary journey in the mist;
It stands by the breakwater,
Watching the swallows flying and sliding on the water surface;
Behind the swallows is the bushy shoal,
Under a gloomy, grey sky,
A red falcon proudly stands;
Over the shoal lies another stream.
In every empty waterway
There is the white egret, waiting;
Another shoal lies behind the stream,
Amidst the barren, brownish, dried brambles
An eagle flaps its wings,
Slowly flying out.
This is the lower stream of Ta Tu Brook,
Cities and factories crowd the banks,
Railway and highway run over the riverbed,
Stream water quietly runs,
Bends into the city,
Taking out dirt,
And flows to the river where the waterfowl dwell;
Before the morning mist disappears,

The nocturnal egrets return from the night;
Swallows, one by one, fly back to the bridge mound;
The blue sandpiper carries on its solitary journey
From the south to the north shore,
Drifting along the waterway, making its dwellings;
In dawn, it stays by the breakwater,
At dusk, it stays by the breakwater,
All winter, its stays by the breakwater.

Early in the morning,
Flocks of bronze-colored sandpipers travel in groups;
They, too, stand by the breakwater,
Their eyes cautiously watching;
Their mates stay around.
Calling, guarding;
They use themselves as the center of the living territory,
Forbidding the intrusion of small swallows.

This is the ecology of the upstream;
Kingfishers fly over the water,
Catching small fish;
River birds dive into shallows
To eat worms;
The wide, thickly foliaged woods by the banks drop down,
Mountain birds chasing each other,
Use their voices to communicate;
They travel and play in the trees,
Their cries all over the stream valley
Dueting constantly with the stream's murmur.

Stream water runs through the space between the cliff rocks and
    woods;
It turns from one mountain range and drops abruptly on another
    range;
The bronze-colored sandpipers traveling in groups
Appear in every section of the waterway,
Using themselves as the center of their living territory,
Crying, guarding,

Telling the world that the stream beneath the wide-leaved woods
   is their home;
Early in the morning,
In the dark, dense center of the timber woods,
A short, crisp, shrieking slides across the sky;
This is where the blue-grass birds reside;
In the ecological areas with mountain brooks and splashing wa-
   terfalls,
Among the spaces of the woods,
There are strange noises;
Maybe the blue-belly pheasant has just left,
Maybe a group of quail are fighting;
Before the sun sets,
They have all finished their jobs of hunting food;
Only the quiet forest is left.

Only the sky of the canyon is left
For the wandering of the clouds,
And the falcons and crows highly swirling as companions,
Swirling, guarding
The origin of a river.

Author's note: Ernest F. Schumacher's *Small Is Beautiful* is a classic that calls for ecologi-
cal balance. This is why I am using the book's title as the title for my poem. I am not
making an ecological research project out of humanity, but instead seek only to trace the
ecology of the birds and a river. The backdrop is Ta Tu Brook, which represents the major
distribution of birds in our province.

Appendix: Names and Titles of Poems in Chinese

Translator's note: the list below includes only the Chinese names and titles of poems appearing in the Contents and the Introduction.

"Abode of the Roaming Immortals"
    遊仙眠地
"Accident, The" 意外
"After Dawn" 曉之外
"After My Fiftieth Birthday" 五十歲以後
"Approaching" 臨近
"Autobiography of a Sloppy Sluggard"
    邋遢自述

Back Waves 後浪
"Beginning of the Day, The" 一天的開始
"Betel Palm Tree, A" 檳榔樹
"Beyond Logic" 邏輯之外
"Blackbird, The" 黑鳥
Blue Star 藍星
Blue Star Poetry Broadside 藍星詩頁
Blue Star Poetry Selections 藍星詩選
Blue Star Weekly 藍星週刊
"Border Gate, The" 關闡
"Brewing Stone, The" 釀酒的石頭
"Bricks" 磚
"Broken Bowl, A" 破碗

"Candle Has Slept in its Own Flame, A"
    一枝臘燭在自己的光焰裏睡着了
"Car, A" 街車
"Case of T'ang Wen-piao, The" 唐文標
    事件
Chan Ch'e 詹澈
Chang Chien 張健

Chang Mo 張默
Chang Ts'o 張錯
Chang Tung-fang 張冬芳
Chang Wo-chun 張我軍
Cheng Ch'ou-yu 鄭愁予
Chi Hsien 紀弦
"Chi Tzu of Yen Ling Hangs up his
    Sword" 延陵季子掛劍
Chiang Hsun 蔣勳
Ch'iao Lin 喬林
Ch'in Tzu-hao 覃子豪
China Times 中國時報
"Chinatown" 唐人街
"Ch'ing-ming Nostalgia" 清明鄉思
Ch'ou Meng-tieh 周夢蝶
"Chrysanthemum and the Sword, The"
    菊花與劍
Chung Li-ho 鍾理和
Chung Ting-wen 鍾鼎文
"Climbing the Mountain" 上山
"Common Song, A" 一般之歌
"Confused" 惘然
"Conversing" 對話
Corridor 長廊
"Crab-legged Flower, The" 蟹爪花
"Cricket and the Machine Gun, The"
    蟋蟀和機關槍

"Decadence of Poetry, The" 詩的沒落
"Death of Aphrodite, The" 阿富羅底之死

Ku Chin Chu 古今注
Kuan Chieh-ming 關傑明
Kuan Kuan 管管
Kuo Ch'iu-sheng 郭秋生
"K'ung-hou Harp Tune" 箜篌引
Kung Lun News 公論報

"Ladder-climbing and Grocery" 爬梯及
    雜物
Lai Ho 賴和
Lamp Worship 拜燈
Lan Ling 藍菱
"Landscape in a Pot" 壺中山水
"Landscape Philosophy" 山水哲學
"Legend of Tea, The" 茶的掌故
"Let's First Review Ourselves" 先檢討我
    們自己吧
"Let the Wind Recite" 讓風朗誦
"Let Us Take Down this Dilapitated
    Temple in Withered Weeds" 請合力
    拆下這座敗草攢中的破舊殿堂
"Letter from Home, A" 家書
Li 笠
Li Jong 麗容
Li Nan 李男
Li Sha 李莎
Li Yu 麗玉
Lien Wen-ch'ing 連溫卿
Lien Ya-t'ang 連雅堂
Lin Fu-erh 林佛兒
Lin Heng-t'ai 林亨泰
Lin Huan-chang 林煥彰
Lin Ling 林冷
"Listening to Red Maples on an Empty
    Mountain" 空山聽楓紅
Literature Quarterly 文學季刊
"Little Girl's Show, A" 小女孩的節目
Liu K'o-hsiang 劉克襄
Lo Chih-ch'eng 羅智成
Lo Ch'ing 羅青
Lo Fu 洛夫
Lo Kuan-chung 羅貫中
Lo Ma 羅馬
Lo Men 羅門

"Lone Swordsman, The" 獨行劍客
"Loneliness" 孤獨
"Lord, Do Not Cross the River" 公無渡河
"Lottery, The" 抽獎
"Lotus" 蓮花
Lupus 天狼星
Lung Tsu 龍族
Lung Ying-chung 龍瑛宗

Mainstream 主流
"Marriage of Mother Goose, The" 鵝媽
    媽要出嫁
May Be 也許
"Meadow Upon the Mercy of Heaven,
    The" 看天田
"Meaning of the New Literature
    Movement, The" 新文學運動的意義
Messages 消息
"Mirror, The" 鏡子
Modern Poetry 現代詩
"Modern Poetry is Long Dead" 僵斃的
    現代詩
"Morning Scene, A" 晨景
"Mother Country" 祖國
"Mountain Barrier" 山圍
"MS Found in a Bottle" 瓶中稿

"Night Flute" 夜笛
"Night Guards" 夜晚衛兵
"Night Song: How to Defend Against
    Tree Shadows, A" 夜歌之一:如何抵抗
    樹影
"No One to Care" 無人照顧
"Nocturne" 夜歌
"Nostalgia" 鄉愁四韻
"Nostalgia" 鄉愁

"Old Liu's Dawn" 老劉的黎明
"Old Woman in Mongkok, An" 旺角一
    老嫗
"One Thousand and One Arabian
    Nights" 一千零一夜
"Opera Songstress, An" 坤伶
Orphan of Asia, The 亞細亞的孤兒
"Outdoor Collections" 門外集

NEO-CONFUCIAN STUDIES

MODERN ASIAN LITERATURE SERIES

Modern Japanese Drama: An Anthology, ed. and tr. Ted T. Takaya. Also in paperback ed.	1979
Mask and Sword: Two Plays for the Contemporary Japanese Theater, Yamazaki Masakazu, tr. J. Thomas Rimer	1980
Yokomitsu Riichi, Modernist, by Dennis Keene	1980
Nepali Visions, Nepali Dreams: The Poetry of Laxmiprasad Devkota, tr. David Rubin	1980
Literature of the Hundred Flowers, vol. 1: *Criticism and Polemics*, ed. Hualing Nieh	1981
Literature of the Hundred Flowers, vol. 2: *Poetry and Fiction*, ed. Hualing Nieh	1981
Modern Chinese Stories and Novellas, 1919–1949, ed. Joseph S. M. Lau, C. T. Hsia, and Leo Ou-fan Lee. Also in paperback ed.	1981
A View by the Sea, by Yasouka Shōtarō, tr. Kären Wigen Lewis	1984
Other Worlds: Arishima Takeo and the Bounds of Modern Japanese Fiction, by Paul Anderer	1984
The Isle Full of Noises: Modern Chinese Poetry from Taiwan, ed. and tr. Dominic Cheung	1986

TRANSLATIONS FROM THE ORIENTAL CLASSICS

Major Plays of Chikamatsu, tr. Donald Keene	1961
Four Major Plays of Chikamatsu, tr. Donald Keene. Paperback text edition	1961
Records of the Grand Historian of China, translated from the Shih chi of Ssu-ma Ch'ien, tr. Burton Watson, 2 vols.	1961
Instructions for Practical Living and Other Neo-Confucian Writings by Wang Yang-ming, tr. Wing-tsit Chan	1963
Chuang Tzu: Basic Writings, tr. Burton Watson, paperback ed. only	1964

STUDIES IN ORIENTAL CULTURE

COMPANIONS TO ASIAN STUDIES

Twelfth Century, tr. Burton Watson. Also in
paperback ed.   1971
A Syllabus of Indian Civilization, by Leonard A. Gordon
and Barbara Stoler Miller   1971
Twentieth-Century Chinese Stories, ed. C. T. Hsia and
Joseph S. M. Lau. Also in paperback ed.   1971
A Syllabus of Chinese Civilization, by J. Mason Gentzler,
2d ed.   1972
A Syllabus of Japanese Civilization, by H. Paul Varley,
2d ed.   1972
An Introduction to Chinese Civilization, ed. John Meskill,
with the assistance of J. Mason Gentzler   1973
An Introduction to Japanese Civilization, ed. Arthur E.
Tiedemann   1974
A Guide to Oriental Classics, ed. Wm. Theodore de Bary
and Ainslie T. Embree, 2d ed. Also in paperback ed.   1975
Ukifune: Love in The Tale of Genji, ed. Andrew Pekarik   1982

INTRODUCTION TO ORIENTAL CIVILIZATION
Wm. Theodore de Bary, Editor

Sources of Japanese Tradition 1958 Paperback ed., 2 vols, 1964
Sources of Indian Tradition   1958 Paperback ed., 2 vols., 1964
Sources of Chinese Tradition 1960 Paperback ed., 2 vols., 1964